Fist
8   ).

Restoration & The Cat

Following publication of the rehearsal script to coincide with the successful Royal Court premiere in July 1981, *Restoration* is now re-published as a Methuen Modern Play in a completely revised definitive edition which takes account of all the changes made during production. Also included for the first time is Nick Bicât's highly praised music for the fourteen songs in the play. 'Edward Bond's *Restoration* towers like a colossus . . . its stylistic wit, moral complexity and theatrical force are of the kind one associates with classic drama'

Michael Billington, *Guardian*

The other play in this volume, *The Cat*, has never been published before. Set in London at the turn of the century, the main characters are cats – with a mouse, a fox and a few dogs and birds completing the cast. It was written as the libretto for an opera by the composer Hans Werner Henze.

The photograph on the front cover is by John Haynes and shows Philip Davis as Bob in the Royal Court 1981 production of Restoration. *The photograph of Edward Bond on the back cover is by Chris Davies.*

by the same author

in Methuen's Modern Plays

SAVED
NARROW ROAD TO THE DEEP NORTH
THE POPE'S WEDDING
LEAR
THE SEA
BINGO
THE FOOL and WE COME TO THE RIVER
THE BUNDLE
THE WOMAN
THE WORLDS with THE ACTIVISTS PAPERS
SUMMER

in the Master Playwrights series

PLAYS: ONE (The Pope's Wedding, Saved, Early Morning)
PLAYS: TWO (Lear, The Sea, Narrow Road to the Deep North,
Black Mass *and* Passion)

also available

THEATRE POEMS AND SONGS
SPRING AWAKENING by Frank Wedekind
(translated by Edward Bond)

Edward Bond

Restoration
&
The Cat

METHUEN · LONDON

Restoration first published in Great Britain in 1981 in the Royal Court Writers series by Eyre Methuen Ltd., 11 New Fetter Lane, London EC4P 4EE. Re-issued in Methuen Modern Plays in this re-set and revised edition in 1982 by Methuen London Ltd.

The Cat first published in 1982 by Methuen London Ltd.

Restoration copyright © 1981, 1982 by Edward Bond

Music for *Restoration* copyright © 1981 by Nick Bicât. The melodies are included at the end of this volume; full orchestration can be obtained from Nigel Brittain, London Management & Representation Ltd, 235 Regent Street, London W1

The Cat copyright © 1982 by Edward Bond

Printed by Richard Clay (The Chaucer Press) Ltd, Bungay, Suffolk

ISBN 0 413 48840 3 (Hardback)
ISBN 0 413 49920 0 (Paperback)

Restoration

A Pastoral

Restoration was first presented at the Royal Court Theatre, London on 21 July 1981, with the following cast:

BOB	Philip Davis
LORD ARE	Simon Callow
FRANK	Nicholas Ball
MR HARDACHE	Wolfe Morris
PARSON	Norman Tyrrell
GABRIEL	John Barrett
MESSENGER	Kit Jackson
GAOLER	Patrick Murray
ROSE	Debbie Bishop
MOTHER, *Mrs Hedges*	Elizabeth Bradley
ANN	Eva Griffith
MRS WILSON	Darlene Johnson
OLD LADY ARE	Irene Handl

Directed by Edward Bond
Music by Nick Bicât
Designed by Hayden Griffin and Gemma Jackson
Lighting by Rory Dempster

England, eighteenth century – or another place at another time

Part One

Part Two

Note on the songs

In the first production of *Restoration* 'Hurrah' was cut from Scene Eight. It would be possible to cut 'Dream Song' from Scene Eleven and sing it between Scenes Ten and Eleven. 'Suddenly' would then have to be cut.

It's a Big Broad Fine Sunny Day

It's a big broad fine sunny day
The black clouds are gonna blow away
It's true that the rockets are aimed in their pits
But they wont be fired, not this time
This time there ain't gonna be any crime
This time we're gonna say no
This time we're gonna be wise guys
And tell the bastards where to go

It's a big broad fine sunny day
It's getting more sunny all the time
It's true that the bombs are stacked in their racks
But we won't load them up, not this time
This time there ain't gonna be no more war
This time we're gonna say no
This time we're gonna be wise guys
And tell the bastards where to go

It's a big broad fine sunny day
It's getting better all the time
And this time the soldiers will not march away
So they won't be shot at, not this time
This time they ain't gonna die for the sods
This time they're gonna say no
This time they're staying here to play
And tell the bastards where to go

It's a big broad fine sunny day
And the sky gets bluer all the time
From now on we'll live in the way that we say
And we won't be told, not this time
This is our world and it's staying that way
This time we're gonna say no
Today we'll live till tomorrow
And tell the bastards where to go

Part One

Scene One

London.
The Park of LORD ARE'*s house.*
ARE *and* FRANK. FRANK *is in livery.*

ARE. Lean me against that great thing.

FRANK. The oak sir?

ARE. Hold your tongue. No no! D'ye want me to appear
drunk? Nonchalant. As if I often spent the day leaning
against an oak or supine in the grass.

FRANK. Your lordship comfortable?

ARE. No scab I am not, if that gives ye joy. Hang my scarf
over the twig. Delicately! – as if some discriminating wind
had cast it there. Stand off. How do I look?

FRANK. Well sir ... how would yer like to look?

ARE. I wore my russet and green of a purpose. Must I sprout
berries before I am at home in the landscape?

FRANK. Not seen your lordship –

ARE. Pox! ye city vermin can't tell the difference between a
haystack and a chimney stack. Wha-ha! I must not laugh,
it'll spoil my pose. Damn! the sketch shows a flower. 'Tis
too late for the shops, I must have one from the ground.

FRANK. What kind sir?

ARE. Rip up that pesky little thing on the path. That'll teach
it to grow where gentlemen walk. (FRANK *offers the
flower.*) Smell it! If it smells too reprehensible throw it
aside. I hate the gross odours the country gives off. 'Tis
always in a sweat! Compare me to the sketch.

FRANK (*checks sketch*). Leg a bit more out.

ARE. Lawd I shall be crippled. *Do* they stand about the
country so? When I pass the boundaries of the town I lower
the blinds in mourning and never go out on my estate for
fear of the beasts.

FRANK. Cows aren't beasts sir.

ARE. The peasants sirrah. Don't mar the sketch with your
great thumbs. I had it drew up by a man renowned for his
landscapes to show me how a gentleman drapes himself
across his fields. That I call a proper use for art. The book
oaf! Well sirrah open it! Must I gaze on the cover as if I
wondered what manner of thing I held in my hand?

FRANK. Any page sir?

ARE. The blanker the better. (*Looks at the page.*) Turn sir.
The poet spilt his ink and scribbled to use it up before it
dried. A poem should be well cut and fit the page neatly as
if it were written by your tailor. The secret of literary style
lies in the margins. Now *that* sir could only have been
written by Lord Lester's tailor, whose favourite colour is
woad. Turn me to something short. Your master is a man
of epigrammatic wit. About your business. I must pine.

FRANK *goes*.

What a poor gentleman I am! Town house and park,
country house and land as far as the eye can see, they tell
me – for I never look out, 'twould remind me how far off
was the town – debts to honour a duke, and broke. So: a
rich bride. Yonder, about to rise over the horizon like a
pillar of smoke, is Mr Hardache, iron founder, ship builder, mine owner and meddler and merchant in men and
much else that hath money in it. With his daughter, who
must have a title and country estate to go with her fortune.
Well marriages have been built on weaker foundations.
The heart changes but pride does not. So here I am set,
imitating the wild man of the woods. An extravagant ges-

ture but I would have the gal love me at sight and be spared
the tedium of courting an iron master's daughter. Faith
boys what would one do: rattle a spoon in a tin mug and call
it a serenade? Peace good soul! You have but to glance up
from this bundle of tasteless moralising – the relief itself
will bring rapture to thy face – and the slut's fate is sealed. I
hope I am not to wait for a change in the season? I shall put
out branches or turn white in a hoar frost.

BOB *enters.*

A swain wanders o'er the landscape.

BOB. Well London here I am! What strange sights I hev seen!
ARE. Why does the fool gawp so impertinently? Lawd it
grins!
BOB. Mornin' my lord.
ARE. Gad it addresseth me! Oaf be off!
BOB. Ay sir, where to?
ARE. Where to? What care I where to? To hell! Wha-ha!
(*Aside.*) Dear heart do not discommode thy complexion. A
raw face is a countrified look but I would not have one even
to gaze on the blazing of the bankruptcy court! Dear gad
my foot is misplaced!
BOB (*aside*). Doo a London gentleman complain when his
foot move? However do they git into bed – or out of it? –
Shall us carry yoo sir?
ARE (*aside*). I am dealing with a harmless lunatic. The iron
people have turned into the avenue. Soon we shall hear
them clank. – Good fellow, take the run of my grounds. Go
and play.
BOB (*aside*). This is a test Bob. Don't git caught out. (*Idea.*)
Drat what a fool I am! That owd rag round your neck hev
hitched yoo up in the bramble! Tell by the look on yoor
face! I'll soon haul yoo out sir!

ARE (*pushing* BOB *away*). Off sir! Back to your bedlam!

BOB. Why sir 'tis Bob – come of age and sent up to serve as yoor man, as laid down in the history of our estate: eldest Hedges boy hev the right to serve his lord. Steward writ an' say he were sendin' me up.

ARE (*aside*). This comes from opening a poetry book. – Sirrah . . . ?

BOB. Bob sir. Or Robert Hedges.

ARE. Bob, yonder is a paddock. Go and graze.

BOB. Graze sir?

ARE. A country lad must know how to graze!

BOB(*aside*). I must learn their ways if I'm to survive. – Ay sir.

ARE. Then graze.

BOB (*shrugs. Aside*). I'll chew three stalks t' show willin'. That'll hev to doo.

> BOB *goes.*

ARE. Yonder comes my money. (*Reads.*)

> HARDACHE *enters.*

HARDACHE. Lord Are.

ARE. La sir ye surprised me!

HARDACHE. My girl's back of the hedge, studyin' the shop window. (*Calls.*) Come daughter, or his lordship'll think you don't know your manners. A retiring lass.

ARE (*aside*). Good. Let her retire to the country and leave London to me.

HARDACHE. You'll soon know her ways. Mind, she has a temper – like her mother. That blessed woman ran my shops like an empire. (*Calls.*) Pst! Come daughter. – She has all the airs of a lady. Learned it from the customers. Not that she works in the shop now, O no! Last week the soup was cold. She hauls the cook in and rows her out in front of the guests till she shakes like a dog being shown the

well. Anything she likes, she must have. Saw a carriage
with a new fancy way of panels – must have. A duchess
with diamonds in her hat – must have. Skrawky pet dog –
must have. Little black maid – one of them too. I don't
begrudge. She's all that's left of her mother to me, barrin' a
few shawls. That good woman worked all her life – till we
had a penny to spend on ourselves and tuppence to mend
the damage – and died at the counter with a slice of dinner
in her hand. We're a family sort of family –

ARE (*aside*). Lawd he'll quote me the jingles on his family
tomb-stones.

HARDACHE. – and I intend to make you part of us!

ARE (*aside*). Pox if I call him father!

ANN (*off*). Pst!

HARDACHE. You call my sweet?

ARE. Fetch her sir – (*Aside*.) ere the ivy grow o'er me.

HARDACHE (*calls*). I'll meet you halfway.

> ANN *comes on downstage and*
> HARDACHE *goes down to her.*

ARE. Not uncomely, but the neglect is beyond redemption!
Style cannot strike at any age like a conversion, its rudi-
ments are learned in the nursery or never. That redness of
cheek might be had off a coster's barrow for ha'pence. But
I'll take her, as she comes with money.

HARDACHE. Well sweetheart? (*By her*.) Hussy you're fit for
nowt but an errand boy but you're my daughter and you'll
marry an earl.

ANN. But father! He's got four limbs and his wind. He could
last for years.

HARDACHE. Shan't I buy good stock?

ANN. O you are a fool father! Lucy married a count with gout
who lasted no more than three months. And Audrey's old
baron died of overeating in a year – and he was no trouble

while he were alive. He chased her round the bed but were too fat to catch her. She lost pounds and looked better after her marriage than she did before – and few girls can say as much!

HARDACHE. Come miss.

ANN. Even that ugly Mary Flint. Her father got her an earl of nowt but twenty-five. But he was so eaten up with the diseases he was born with and those he'd acquired – and mad, she had three doctors testify to him before she signed the settlement – that when they came into church the poor parson didn't know whether to turn to the marriage ceremony or the burial of the dead. He were right too: they'd no sooner left the church than they had to go back in for the internment. She went with the peeling and came back with the tolling. But what have you ever done for me father?

HARDACHE. Presently my lord!

ANN. Can't you find one in a wheel-chair or at least on a crutch, so a body might hope? Did you enquire if the family die young? No – you are a thoughtless man father. And what does it matter that he has land in the country? You know I abominate the place.

ARE. Pray unhitch me.

ANN. Can't we leave him to see if he hang?

HARDACHE (*to* ARE). My daughter's too well brought up to touch a gentleman's linen in public. (*Releases* ARE.) Now sir.

ARE. Servant ma'am.

ANN. Good day sir.

ARE. Let me show you the grounds. A few roses, a plantation, a pretty forest, the best kept wilderness, and a jungle in the hothouse. We will not bother with the water gardens – a puddle compared to the lakes of Hilgay!

ANN (*aside*). Perhaps he's prone to accidents. – Did the scarf wound you sir?

ARE. Wound! Fwa! when I take a toss out hunting the ground cracks.

ANN (*aside*). Well, best know the worst. He's still the first box at the play, eating out in great houses, orchestral balls. I'll be presented at court and dance with the prince the second time he asks – the first time I'll be in one of my pets and give him a great yawn.

ARE (*aside*). Cupid has lodged his shaft. I'll beat up my price and set her onto that old maker of cinders. That light in the eye of a slut or a countess is the true lust for money.

> ARE *and* ANN *go*.

HARDACHE (*calls*). Rose! – You youngsters go and look at the flowers. I'll wait up at the house.

> ROSE *comes in*.

Call me if the hussy runs off. He can fondle her hand and rub up against her – but nowt else.

ROSE. Yes sir.

> HARDACHE *goes*. BOB *comes on. He has already met* ROSE.

BOB. Shall us follow?

ROSE. No.

BOB. Hev you notice the sky is gold? Knew the streets ont paved with it. If I was towd the sky was I ont believe that neither.

ROSE. The sun shines on the smoke.

BOB. Lawd. I'm Bob. What yoo called gal?

ROSE. Rose.

BOB. Will yoo show us London Rose?

ROSE. Won't get time for sightseein'.

BOB. Ont mind that, rather kip busy. But I intend to see the churches an' palaces an' docks an' markets. Whey-hay!

Rose if yoor lady an' my lord git wed, as yoo say, us'll see a lot of each other, which us'll like. Make a bargain: yoo say everytime I goo wrong.

ROSE. That'll keep me busy. You run up here to get away from some poor cow carryin' your bastard.

BOB. Thass a lie! Ont ought a charge a chap with that!

ROSE. Keep yer shirt on.

BOB. Thass all right then, s'long as we know. – Look at the way *they* go on! Could drive a cart between 'em. Treat a Hilgay gal like that she'd reckon there was summat wrong with her. I'll show yoo how that ought to be done. First yoo take the gal's hand an' walk her up an' down. Bin a hard week so she soon git tired an' goo a bit slow.

ROSE. She's not goin' too far. She'll probably have to come back on 'er own.

BOB. He's a thoughtful chap so he steer her to a bank an' pat the grass. 'Take the weight off yoor feet gal'.

ROSE. No, I'm wearing my best dress.

BOB. Yoo hev t'say yes or I can't show yoo how to doo it. 'Look' he say 'yoo're a pretty gal' an' he give her a (*Picks up* ARE's *flower*.) Lady's Smock. Then yoo give him a kiss.

ROSE. Why?

BOB. You hev to!

ROSE. Why?

BOB. God yoo're a disconcertin' woman gal! Thass considered very rude in Hilgay. Yoo hev the flower, yoo hev t'kiss – or thass bad luck for both parties for a whole year. Ought to give us some luck Rose – (*Kisses her.*) on my first day in London.

Roses (BOB)

I lay a red rose on your breast
A red rose on a dusky flower

It rises and falls in the scent of your mouth
Your breath is a breeze that blows
In the silent world where the ice walls tower
And melts the snows to sparkling streams
And brings the swallows home from the south ...
In the scent of your breath and from the rose
The petals open and fall apart
Scatter and lie upon your heart
And there I lay my head in repose
I kiss the petals
They stir and close
Close to the secret bud again
The bud in which are hidden away
The breezes of spring
The gentle rain
And the warmth of a summer's day.

Scene Two

Hilgay.
The Hall.
Porch.
MOTHER *and* PARSON.

MOTHER. Upset yoo ont let 'em parade in a line. Ont often
git a bit of fun.
PARSON. Let them work – that's what his lordship would
wish to see.

> ARE *and* ANN *enter.*
> FRANK *goes in and out with boxes.*

ARE. Faw! The dust! Parson ye have emptied your graveyard
on my doorstep!
PARSON. My lord I shall pray for rain.

ARE *enters the house.*

ANN. Every bone in my body's broken. My stomach's changed places with my liver. (*To* FRANK.) Mind that box man!

PARSON. My lady welcome to Hilgay. We asked a blessing on the wedding –

ANN (*to* FRANK). Get them away from his feet!

PARSON. – and would gladly have held the service at St John's. His lordship's father was christened, married and buried there, as were –

ANN (*to* FRANK). Don't slam it man!

FRANK. 'S heavy.

ANN. So will my fist be round your chops!

MOTHER. M'lady, Mrs Hedges yoor housekeeper.

ANN. Make someone keep an eye on the carriage! Who are those ruffians loitering round the back?! Be off! They'll steal my new things!

BOB *comes on. His livery is the same as* FRANK'S.

PARSON. My lady the parish has had an outbreak of method-ists! On Sunday I took the horses from their stalls and drove the fanatics through the lanes. 'Tis no boast to say that on Monday the beasts were so weary 'twas painful to lead them to the shafts.

ANN *goes in. The* PARSON *follows*

BOB. Ma.

MOTHER. Boy yoo look smart.

They can't embrace because BOB *is putting down a parcel.*

BOB. Keepin' well?

MOTHER. Gittin' by. Dad's out the back, brought him up to the house. She the sort a creature she looks like?

BOB. Yes if thass cow.

MOTHER. I can handle cows.

BOB. Tell dad I'll be out soon's I git his lordship straight.

BOB goes in. MOTHER *examines the luggage.*

MOTHER. Huh load of old stuff. Ont need that here.

ROSE comes in. MOTHER *straightens up and sees her.*

MOTHER. Eek!

ROSE. Mrs Hedges.

MOTHER. Thought the devil catch me pryin'. Give me a turn gal.

ROSE. I'm the lady's maid.

MOTHER. Ay. Heard the London servants was getting black. Sorry I shouted my dear. The house is my territory by right and conquest. What goo on outside come under the steward or head gardener – I ont responsible for their lawlessness. Mr Phelps is the parson when yoo goo to church – which yoo better had, doo they complain – an' the magistrate when yoo goo to court – which you better hand't. Yoor regular duties come under her ladyship but anything relatin' to the runnin' of the house come under me: where yoo sit at table, upkeep of yoor room an' any set-to yoo hev with the servants – I'm the law, an' the mercy if yoo're lucky. That clear my pet? Disorder's unprofitable all round.

ROSE. Ta I like to know where I am.

MOTHER. Git her ladyship settled like a good gal and come down to my kitchen. Must be famished. (*Idea.*) Yoo ont eat special?

ROSE. No.

MOTHER. Jist as well cause we ont hev it. I'll find yoo summat tasty.

BOB comes in and embraces ROSE.

MOTHER. You two know each other.

ROSE. We're married Mrs Hedges.

MOTHER. Married? Well. (*Pause for thought.*) Black cow give milk same as white cow. They say black the grate an' the fire burn better. Still, god doo goo in for surprises. Hev a daughter-in-law! Well send a lad to London he's bound to come back different. Could hev got someone to write a letter. I'd hev got it read.

ROSE. Their weddin' kept us busy.

BOB. We're very happy ma.

MOTHER. They all are t' start with, otherwise they ont git married. Well. Us'll hev to –. Fancy hevin' a daughter! Take a minute to git use to! Need a double bed. I'll invite both on yoo to a glass of wine in my pantry. Settle her ladyship first. Don't want a paddy on her first day in the house.

ROSE. Let the cow wait. I haven't had five minutes with Bob all day.

> FRANK *comes in.*

FRANK. Nobs gone up?

ROSE. Yeh.

FRANK. Dump ennit? Cruel to animals keepin' 'em here. All the trees look alike. Don't yer get lost? 'Fraid to stick me head out the winder 'case I can't find me way back. Do all right though! What's the talent like? Smart lad down from London, good looker, spin a yarn, knocked about a bit – what? Answer to a maiden's prayer. Yoo bin prayin' ma? 'Ere, yoo speak English or do animal imitations like Bob?

MOTHER. Mrs Hedges the housekeeper. Pleased to make yoor acquaintance Mr . . . ?

FRANK. Frank love, I dispense with the title: don't pull rank. All them bulls an' cows runnin' abaht in the altogether – gals must go round ready for it all the time. But I don't fancy them fields. Now a back alley's been the scene of many of my –

BOB. Pay no notice.

FRANK. Speaks English though don't she Bobby. Well sort of. She yer ma? Pleased to meet yer Mrs Hedges.

MOTHER. If they bought a donkey for its bray I could sell yoo to the lord mayor. Git all that stuff out my porch –

FRANK. Your ma gettin' at me Bobby?

MOTHER. – before we break our necks.

FRANK. Ask me, put it back on the coach. Don't see madam stickin' this caper.

MOTHER. Yoo jist git them cases –

FRANK. Not me Mrs Hedges. I'm the outdoor servant. Bob's indoors. I fetch an' carry outside – *an'* not all this junk. In London it's letters, presents done up in little boxes, pick up from the florists, or follow yer lady when she's shoppin'. If this was London an' his lordship stood on that line I'd have to clean the front of his boots an' Bobby'd have to clean the back.

Song of Learning (FRANK)

For fifty thousand years I lived in a shack
I learned that a shack is not a place to live in
For fifty thousand years I built mansions for men of wealth
That's how I learned to build a mansion for myself

For fifty thousand years I hammered and toiled
All that I made was taken away from my hands
For fifty thousand years I ran factories for men of wealth
That's how I learned to run a factory for myself

For fifty thousand years I waited at table
I learned to cook and how to unbottle the wine
For fifty thousand years I watched rich men tuck in like swine
From now on the food is gonna be mine

For fifty thousand years I printed their books
I learned how to read by looking over their shoulder
For fifty thousand years I built libraries for men of wealth
That's how I learned to write the books I need for myself.

For fifty thousand years I fought in their wars
I died so often I learned how to survive
For fifty thousand years I fought battles to save their wealth
That's how I learned to know the enemy myself

For fifty thousand years I gave them my life
But in all that time they never learned how to live
For fifty thousand years I was governed by men of wealth
Now I have learned to make the laws I need for myself

I have known pain and bowed before beauty
Shared in joy and died in duty
Fifty thousand years I lived well
I learned how to blow up your hell.

Scene Three

Hilgay.
The Hall.
LADY ARE'*s Drawing Room.*
ANN *with a book.*

ANN. Last night I had a wonderful dream. We were walking
arm in arm. A perfect day. Suddenly rain bucketed down.
We sheltered under a tree. Wind howled in the branches –
and a bolt of lightning hit it. It crashed down, struck my
husband on the head and drove him straight into the
ground like a hammer striking a nail. He weren't there!
Vanished! Killed and buried at one blow! I wasn't even

brushed. Then the sun came out. Well it would, wouldn't it? And Lucy and Peg – my best school chums – rode up in a carriage sat on top of a great mountain of my luggage. And I'm whisked off to a gala given by royalty at Covent Garden for all the people to celebrate my release. Ee I was that happy!

ARE *comes in. He carries bills.* ANN *curtsies.*

ARE. If ye've crooked your ankle try cow liniment ma'am.
ANN (*aside*). I shan't be provoked.– O what a lovely thing!
ARE. What ma'am?
ANN. That jacket.
ARE. D'ye like it? My plum red. Ye begin to have taste.
ANN. And that other thing round your neck!
ARE. The cravat? Pox ma'am 'tis a disaster! Odious! My oaf of a man left it out and hid the rest. Had I been visiting anyone but your ladyship I'd have stayed in my room.
ANN. Oh no it's a picture!
ARE. Well insult me to my face. It but confirms that your tailor's bills are wasted on you. Pox ma'am, one of us must give up this damned foolish habit of followin' the fashion – and I'm damned sure it ain't me. I'll get something from the marriage! Ye have the title and may be thankful that unlike the fashion that has not changed in the last six hundred years and will not in the next. When my mother departed this house in haste she abandoned her wardrobe. Hitherto it was a supply for dusters but ye may sort out something to wrap in. Her taste was execrable but it will do for the servants.
ANN. Your lordship will tease.
ARE. Tease ma'am? I never tease about fashion. On that subject I am always serious – and correct. Well today ye're pleased to ogle me like an ape, but ye commonly find my society tedious –

ANN (*aside*). At last he's said something I agree with and I can't tell him.

ARE. – and as I never willingly discomfit a lady I'll relieve ye of it. I depart for London within the week to see to the refurbishments ordered to my house to console me at the time of my wedding. I told the designer the dining room should be apple green. He hath sent me a sample. If any apple were ever that colour Adam would not have been tempted and mankind would not have fallen. Next I asked for a crimson drawing room. 'Tis a modest wish. The rogue hath sent me a specimen of wincing pink – the colour of his cheeks when I kick him from the house.

ANN. O lawd sir why wait a week? I'll pack my things and we may be off –

ARE. 'Twas agreed ye spent six months in the country learning manners. A wholely optimistic time but a newly married man is fond and believes in miracles – as well he may. Six months. 'Tis not my fault the designer hath gone colour-blind in one. Ye stay.

ANN. But sir how can I learn manners here? What refinement can I get from a duck pond?

ARE. Try the parson's sister. But keep her off Deuteronomy. She once went to Bath. The visit was brief but she heard a concerto. She will hum ye the tune if ye ask her – and indeed, I believe, if ye do not. I assure ye that if in six months ye are totally transformed none will be more thankful than I.

ANN. Oh you pig! Pig!

ANN *throws a book at him. He picks it up.*

ARE (*reads*). 'The Duchess of Winchelsea's Guide to Conduct with Notes on Presentation at Court and Selected Subjects for Polite Conversation with Examples of Repartee, Condolence and so forth.' I see ye have read it. Winchelsea is an illiterate hag whose conduct would have her expelled from a madhouse. Repartee? – no one talks to her but Lord Lester and his repartee is as sparkling as a judge passing sentence of death. Ho! ye have much to learn.

ANN. I'll learn you this my lad! Your title lasted six hundred years but it'll likely die with you! I shan't enter your bedroom till you can hear the singing at Covent Garden when the window's shut!

ARE. Fie ma'am! I intend to bequeath posterity the memorial of my life not some snot-nosed brat! If I have a boot or cape named after me – as I hope to have a hat – I shall be content. I tell ye ma'am, your father palmed me dud coin. I've had ladies swell for far less labour and far more pleasure.

ANN. You monster! You promised me –

ARE. Ma'am a gentleman will promise anything to avoid quarrelling in church with a parson.

ANN. Not his vows you ape! My vows! You promised me theatres, parties, dining in palaces, footmen, clothes. I was to meet the prince. I didn't expect you to keep all your promises. But you haven't kept one!

ARE. Why ma'am if a gentleman kept his promises society would fall apart. I promised? Forsooth and is that not enough? Have ye not had the pleasure of the promise? Your feet tapped when I promised you the opera! Your mouth watered when I promised you diamonds! Your knees shivered when I promised you the prince! What happiness I gave you! I denied you nothing. I was a prodigal of promise. Why ma'am have ye not noticed I promise all the time? I am a christian. I go about the world scattering promises on the suffering and destitute. Would ye have me hard-hearted and not promise my fellow man in his misery? Fwaw! Be silent ma'am! Ye asked to learn and ye shall. I promised! Ungrateful gal was that not enough but that now you must have the promises kept? What fool doesn't know that promises are better not kept? 'Tis plain folly in a gentleman to keep his word. I verily believe that is the cause of half the world's miseries. What surer way have we to drive our friends to despair? I shall not be so cruel to any man that it can ever be said I kept one promise I made him. Why I promise ye the stars! The Atlantic ocean! There is no limit to my generosity! I promise ye the moon! Now ma'am must I keep my promise? Do ye not know that every man who ever sighed has promised the moon to someone? Will ye all go a-squabbling for it? Ma'am I wonder that ye can live in this world at all with a mind so unschooled in polite society. The sundial is promised the sun – yet is content to read the shadows! And hath it not snowed in June? I shall now promise to pay your tailor and if he hath wit enough to thread a needle he'll know what that promise is worth.

ARE *goes*.

ANN (*calls*). Rose! O I have a new purpose to go to London. *Revenge*. I'll shame him at the greatest soirée of the season. I'll wait till the prince, to further his cause with me, is about to offer him some high office and then say in a whisper loud enough to wake the postilions in the street 'Nay, sire, make him an admiral and your chance of a liaison is gone' then sit back and watch him cry in some magnificent palace.

ROSE *comes in*.

ANN. Can you do voodoo?
ROSE. Voodoo?
ANN (*indicating a jewel*). I'll give you my pin.
ROSE. No ma'am.
ANN. O you heartless brazen liar! I'm sure your mother

taught you. It comes naturally to you people. You cut a chicken's neck and say spells.

ROSE. I don't believe in all that.

ANN. If only someone would help me! I tried sticking pins in a doll when we were married. This house is haunted. A girl was bricked up for carrying on out of wedlock. She comes out of the wall of a morning and wails. I don't have to keep you on when I get to London. Black girls aren't the novelty they were Miss Will-when-she-wants-to. You're two a penny. Rose you could dress up as the ghost and threaten him.

ROSE. My husband wouldn't let me.

ANN. We shan't tell him.

ROSE. Too risky. If his lordship found out he'd sack me and my husband.

ANN. Very well. You had your warning. I'll do it myself.

Dream (ROSE)

I sit in a boat and float down a river of fire
The boat is cool – it doesn't burn in the heat
The flames hide us from the banks
Where the whiteman aims his gun
The boat sails safely on
The whitemen rage and stamp their feet
Then the fire flows up the banks and into the trees
The whitemen run and the fire comes out
The river of fire chases them till they fall
To their knees and crawl about in the flames
The river burns everything that stands in its path
Forests and men are all consumed in its wrath
   I am black
   At night I press through the land unseen
   Though you lie awake
   My smile is as sharp as the blade in my hand

But when the fire is spent
The ground is not scorched
The trees are not charred
The land is green in the morning dew
The cattle passed through the flames yet are not dead
Only the whiteman's bones are black
Lying by his burned out tanks
Now cattle graze the river banks
Men and women work in the fields
All that they grow they own
To be shared by old and young
In the evening they rest
And the song of freedom is sung
   I am black
   At night I pass through the land unseen
   Though you lie awake
   My smile is as sharp as the blade in my hand
   The venom does not kill the snake.

Scene Four

Hilgay.
The Hall.
'The Thieving Scene'.
Workroom.
Chest and chairs.
MOTHER *and* ROSE.
MOTHER *cleans silver and* ROSE *sews.*

MOTHER. Ont lose things. Thass took. Knife an' fork. Be the
   devil to pay. Yoo can write it in my Loss Book so I ont hev
   to bother parson. Yoor mother alive gal?
ROSE. Yes. She was a slave. Her boss got rich and came to

England and their kids cried so they brought her with them.

FRANK *comes in dazed, exhausted and filthy.*

MOTHER. Mornin' 'outside'. Don't mess in here, nough t' clean up.

FRANK. Bloody hole! In London yer work all hours but yer not an animal. More'n two parcels an' yer call a porter! But what am I here? Muck out the yard. Heave pig shit. Ashamed t' smell meself. If I got back to London I wouldn't get a job in this state. Never wash the muck off me hands. Like bein' branded! Night time I'm wore out. Creep into bed. If I had a bird I'd fall asleep on her. Fat chance of that! (*Without humour:*) Their fellas guard 'em with pitchforks. O Rosie I'm so tired I could cry. Why did we ever leave London?

MOTHER. Jist upset his-self.

ROSE (*cradles* FRANK's *head*). Hush.

He instantly falls asleep.

MOTHER. Yoo London folks are a proper laugh. Bit a hard work hev him cryin' like a babby.

ROSE. He's not used to workin' in the yard.

MOTHER. Git used, same's everyone else.

ROSE. He don't mind working with his hands but that's *all* he does now. Likes to use his brains. He's smart – aren't you Frank? (*Shakes him awake.*)

FRANK (*as if waking from a dream*). Hens cacklin'. Cows roarin'. Horses kickin'. Dogs snarlin'. Bloody great curs! Dogs in London sit on cushions an' say thanks when yer feed 'em. These bloody mastiffs 'd rip yer hand off. Me nerves are in shreds.

ROSE. Sit down.

FRANK (*sits in* ROSE's *chair*). Ta Rose. Yer a saint.

Wood Song (MOTHER)

The wooden cradle the wooden spoon
The wooden table the wooden bed
The wooden house the wooden beam
The wooden pulpit the wooden bench
The wooden hammer the wooden stair
The wooden gallows the wooden box
The iron chain the brass locks
The human toil the earthly span
These are the lot of everyman
The winds that drive the storms that blast
For everyman the die is cast
    All you who would resist your fate
    Strike now it is already late

MOTHER. My family polished this silver so long the pattern's rub off. Mother say 'Fruits pluck and birds flown'. Her mother an' her mother polished 'em in the winder to git the best light. Howd 'em up an' see the colour of your eyes in 'em – then they're clean. Show the babbys their face upside down in the spoon, turn it round an' they're the right way up: one of the wonders of the world. Kip 'em quiet for hours. Saw my face in that when I were a kid. Mother say 'When yoor turn come, yoo clean 'em as good as that gal'. She's bin in the churchyard twenty years. Wash 'em an' set 'em an' clean 'em after but ont eat off 'em once.

ROSE. Use 'em tonight. Have a feast. I'll lay the table an' the parson won't have to pray for yer.

MOTHER. Don't be cheeky. Bad 'nough clean 'em t' let others make 'em dirty. What I want goo dirtyin' 'em meself for? Food taste jist as good off mine.

    BOB *comes in.*

BOB. Parson's called.

MOTHER. Goo upstairs?

BOB. Yip. Says a prayer – an' then off up to see her ladyship.

MOTHER. Git his glass of wine out on the hall table. Allus set it ready. Old man his age need summat t' set him up.

MOTHER *goes out.*

BOB. Look at that lazy sod.

Takes some tape from the work-basket and begins to tie FRANK *to the chair at the ankles, knees and elbows.*

ROSE. What's that for?

BOB. Teach the lazy pig to sit.

ROSE. He's wore out. (*Helps* BOB *with the tying.*) Go easy. I have to account for every inch of that.

BOB. 'He's wore out'. So 'm I dooin' his work. Truss up lovely me old darlin'. There! Bet he's hevin' all sorts of dreams. Ont know whass in store.

FRANK *opens both eyes.*

FRANK. Bob. Undo me.

BOB. Ont fill the horse trough.

FRANK. Did. Buggers drunk it to cause a ruck. I'll fill it up again. Come on, don't get us into trouble.

BOB. Whass a matter boy? That old chair so fond of yoo it ont let yoo goo.

FRANK. Rose.

ROSE. He'll pay later.

BOB. Ho-ho a bit of hankypanky?

MOTHER *comes in.*

MOTHER. There. Thass set on the table with the saucer on top. Keep the flies out.

FRANK (*trying to stand*). Come on Bob. It's no joke.

BOB (*tickling*). Ickle-wickle piggy goo to market. Ickle-wickle
piggy stay at home. This ickle piggy goo wee-wee-wee!

FRANK. Git off! Bloody lunatic! Don't muck abaht. Me foot
hurts, the blood's cut off.

BOB. Whass the difference, yoo ont use it?

MOTHER. Spoon gone.

ROSE. Can't have. Count 'em.

MOTHER. Can't count. Tell it's gone by the pattern. Knife,
fork – where's the spoon? Who's bin in?

FRANK. Well I'm clear. I was tied up and fast asleep.

MOTHER. Bob yoo ont got it?

BOB. No.

MOTHER. Rose? Hev to ask. It's my job. Easy git swep off by
yoor skirt. Look in the pocket.

ROSE. Don't be daft.

MOTHER. Look.

ROSE (*looks*). No.

FRANK (*wriggles*). This is bloody stupid. Parson nipped in on
his way up. Yer left it in the cupboard. (*Stands.*) Rose get
this off.

MOTHER. Turn his pockets out.

FRANK. Now wait a minute! How could I do it? Trussed up
like a chicken.

MOTHER. Could hev took it afore.

FRANK. Well I ain't.

MOTHER. Bob.

FRANK (*jerks*). Now look here. I'm not havin' this.

MOTHER. I'll hev to look.

FRANK. Don't accuse me Mrs Hedges. Yer didn't use that
tone to them.

MOTHER. I know they ont took it –

FRANK. O do yer!

MOTHER. – and I'm me own judge a character. Ask to see in
yoor pockets, yoo ont hide nothin' yoo ont make a fuss.

FRANK. You'd make a fuss if yer was bloody tied up. What yer do round here to prove yer innocent? Float in the pond?

MOTHER. I lose my silver I lose my job. Out that yard 'fore I turn round. Ont git another job with a bad name.

BOB. Hand it over.

FRANK. Look son – get this bloody chair off or I'll break every bone in yer –

BOB. All right I believe yoo: yoo ont took it.

FRANK. Ta. Now undo these bloody –

BOB. So we'll jist look in yoor pockets to satisfy ma.

FRANK (*tries hitting the chair on the floor*). This has bloody well gone –

ROSE. Let him go!

ROSE *tries to untie* FRANK. BOB *moves her aside.*

BOB. I'll settle this Rose.

FRANK. Keep off son! I warn yer! I'll bloody cripple yer! Treat me like an animal, I'll be one!

MOTHER. Grab him Bob! He ont got the strength to hurt a fly!

BOB. Us'll hev to see Frank.

FRANK. Look I didn't take it – an' what if I had? Thass my wages – by agreement. I get paid bugger all. Why? 'Cause in London I get tips. Take a letter get a tip. Keep yer wits open an' there's plenty of ways to pick up a bit on the side. All yer pick up here's the shit on yer boots!

BOB *tries to search* FRANK. FRANK *spins and tries to defend himself with the chair legs.* BOB *and* FRANK *fight.*

BOB. Quick mum.

BOB *grabs the chair and forces* FRANK *to sit.* FRANK *struggles and jerks.*

BOB. Ont help boy: truss up like a rabbit.

> MOTHER *tries to search* FRANK.

MOTHER. Howd him steady! He's gooin' like –
FRANK. Bitch! I'll kick yer bloody – smash yer bloody –
MOTHER. Beast! Beast! Beast!
ROSE. Stop it! All of yer! Yer like kids.

> ROSE *starts to untie* FRANK. *She releases his arm. He takes the spoon from his pocket and holds it out.*

FRANK. There's yer spoon. I hope it chokes yer.
MOTHER (*takes the spoon*). Any damage t' that chair make it worse.

> FRANK *begins to untie himself.* ROSE *helps him. Suddenly* BOB *turns the chair upside down.* FRANK's *feet are in the air and his head is on the ground.* BOB *jerks the chair.*

BOB. Where yoo hid the rest?
FRANK. That's the lot. Crowd round here it's a wonder there's anythin' left to nick.

> BOB *lets the chair fall flat on its back on the floor.* FRANK *agsain begins to untie himself.*

BOB. I'll search his loft.
MOTHER. Git Ronnie off the field an' tie him up proper. I'll tell his lordship we've bin thief-catchin'. Parson's happen lucky, so I ont hev to send out for a magistrate.
FRANK. Hold on. Yer got the spoon. That's the end of it.
MOTHER. Us'll tell boy.
ROSE. Don't be daft, mother. There's no harm done. Frank'll go and get the knife an' fork – (*To* FRANK.) an' everythin' else yer took – (*To* MOTHER.) an' yer can put it back. (*To* BOB.) Yer ruined my tape. Who's paying for that?

FRANK. It's just the knife an' fork – god's honest.

BOB. Us'll hev to tell.

ROSE. What's the good of that?

BOB. Ten't a question of good. Question of law. Ont break it us-self, an' if someone else do: we stay on the right side an' tell. 'S only way. He's been stealin' for years. Steal himself if it had any value.

MOTHER. Fine Christian I'd be turning him loose on my neighbours. He'd hev t'steal to live on the road.

FRANK. Yer have to steal in my job if yer wanna live. Yer fetch an' carry for 'em, pick 'em up, get 'em upstairs, put 'em to bed, clean up the spew. Stands to reason they drop anythin' – it's yourn. That's only right. Chriss! yer go through their pockets out of self-respect! Give it back, they'd drop it again or lose it gamblin'.

ROSE. For chrissake Bob. They hang yer for stealin'.

FRANK. Gawd.

MOTHER. Could of thought of that. If he was hungry I'd hev understood.

FRANK. Look forget it an' I'll scarper. Down the road an' yer'll never see me ugly mug again. Vanish. Now that's somethin' to look forward to eh? No hard feelings. (*Finishes untying himself, stands and offers his hand.*) Say cheerio ma? (*No response. Offers his hand to* BOB.) Come on old son. Don't upset Rose. She didn't know yer could be like this.

BOB. Ont trust yoo to goo through the gate: yoo'd nick it.

FRANK. Gawd you peasants drive a hard bargain. Stickin' pigs, twistin' necks, carvin' balls off calves – no wonder they treat people like animals. (*To* ROSE.) They after a cut? How much?

ROSE (*to* BOB). That lot can afford a bit of silver. Chriss the work they've got out of him, he deserves it.

MOTHER. Can't Rose, only do us a disservice.

ROSE. Please.

BOB. Yoo ont understand. I hev to take care of yoo now as well as ma.

FRANK. Gawd gal yer married a right little hypocrite there. Nasty little punk. Rotten little git. Arse-crawlin' little shit –

BOB. Thass enough of that before my mother.

> BOB *struggles with* FRANK. MOTHER *opens the lid of the chest and* FRANK *is bundled in.* BOB *closes and bolts the lid.*

Soon settled his hash.

FRANK (*inside*). It's a madhouse!

BOB. Yoo stay quiet an' think up a good excuse.

MOTHER. Phew he git me hot!

> FRANK *starts to kick and punch inside the chest.*

MOTHER. Ont yoo harm that chest boy! He's a proper vandal!

BOB (*aims a kick at the chest*). That ont help. Doo yoorself a mischief!

FRANK (*inside*). Rotten bastards!

BOB (*to* MOTHER). Git parson an I'll git the rope. Rose yoo wait outside, ont stay an' be contaminated by his filth.

FRANK (*inside*). Filthy rotten swine! Shit. Rotten sod. God rot yer yer bastard!

> BOB, MOTHER *and* ROSE *go.* FRANK *rattles the lid, trying to shake it open. Then he tries to knock off the end of the chest by kicking at it violently with both feet together.*

FRANK (*inside*): O gawd they'll hang me. (*Thump.*) Please. Why did I come to this madhouse? (*Thump.*) Please Bob. Bastard. (*Thump.*) Can't stand bein' shut up! Go off me head! (*Violent shower of footfalls on the end of the chest.*)

ROSE *has come in slowly. She stands and watches the chest.*

FRANK (*inside*). Can't breathe! Help! I'll die! (*Shakes the lid with his hands, then tramples his feet on the end of the chest.*) Never do it again pal. Promise. I learned my lesson. O please Bob.

> *Kicking and struggling, changing to regular thumping, and all the while he groans.* ROSE *goes to the chest and gently sits on it. Immediately* FRANK *is still.*

FRANK (*inside*). Bob? The spoon fell on the floor an' I was tempted. Honest. I know it's wrong but I –. No no, it's dark Bob, I'm confused. Listen. I'll tell the truth. I took it to get me own back see? You had yer head down tyin' me feet. I winked at Rose. She'll tell yer. O dear Bob yer fell for a trick there. We're gonna laugh. Come on old sport.

ROSE. Frank.

FRANK (*inside*). Rose.

ROSE. Listen carefully. Yer life depends on it. I'll let yer out –

FRANK (*inside*). O bless yer –

ROSE. – if yer do what I say. Hide in the yard in the little barn till it's dark. Then go. Stay off the road an' keep to the hedges. Yer –

FRANK (*inside*). No, I'll scarper as fast as I –

ROSE. Listen. If yer go on the road now yer'll git caught. Where's the knife an' fork?

FRANK (*inside*). Rose what if they search the –

ROSE. Promise or I won't let yer out.

FRANK (*inside*). Promise.

> ROSE *stands and unbolts the chest.* FRANK *opens the lid and steps out.*

FRANK. Yer darlin'!

ROSE. I'll get the stuff from yer loft.

FRANK. Keep it angel! I'll help meself!

> FRANK *grabs the rest of the silver, drops some, grabs it again but still leaves a few pieces.* ROSE *watches him.*

ROSE. O Frank.

> FRANK *runs out.* ROSE *shuts the chest, bolts it and sits on it.* BOB *comes in with a heavy rope. He goes to the chest and* ROSE *stands.*

BOB (*bangs lid with the flat of his hand*). Gooin' to open yoor lid Frank. Yoo let me tie yoo up. No language – parson'll think thass Hebrew an' hev to look it up. Now then, git ready. (*Opens the lid.*) Ont git far.

ROSE. Yer like a stranger. I don't know yer.

BOB. Seem hard but it's for the best. Meddle in somethin' like this ruin yoor whole life. We think of us, can't afford to think of no one else. Hard times but we got jobs, we could be happy – but we ont if we meddle. He took the risk, now he hev to pay. Ont no way out of that.

Song of the Calf (BOB)

You take the calf to the slaughtering shed
It smells the sweat and blood and shit
It breaks its halter and runs through the lanes
The hollering men run after it

It snorts in the fresh clean morning air
It bellows and lows and tosses its head
And after it with sticks and ropes
Come the hollering men from the slaughtering shed

It reaches the town and runs through the streets
It tries to hide but the children shout
It turns at bay and trembles and groans
The hollering children have found it out

It scatters the mob and flees the town
It stops to rest in a quiet lane
Then peacefully strolls back home to its field
And enters the wooden gate again

And there stand the men from the slaughtering shed
In a circle with sticks and a halter and chain
They seize the calf and fetter it fast
And lead it back to the butcher again

For though it run and bellow and roar
The calf will be tied to the slaughterhouse door
The butcher will cut its throat with his knife
It will sink to its knees and bleed out its life

The morning is over, the work is done
You eat and drink and have your fun
The butcher is sharpening his knife today
Do you know – do you care – who will get away?

BOB. Best git started.

ROSE (*points*). He helped himself again.

BOB (*stares*). Rose yoo git us into terrible trouble.

ROSE. If yer catch him he'll tell – anythin' to get back at you. Let's hope he gets away.

BOB. Well thass a rum un! I come to tie up a thief an I hev to help him git off! (*Tugs the rope between his hands in bewilderment and frustration.*)

ROSE. He's hiding in the yard in the little barn. I'll take him some grub later on. My mother told me what the slaves do. The owners never search the backyards, go tearin' down the road, even the dogs – glad to be off the chain. Some of the overseers go mad – off their head – bound to if yer go round with a whip all day – an' start killin' the blacks. One or two a year, then one a month. Use the whip so it's legal – well it may be against the law but the whites run that. So

the blacks scarper or wait till it's their turn. Yer didn't
know yer'd married all that. Me mother said stay quiet an'
wait for the chance: it'll come. Yer were all rushin' round
shoutin'. So I waited quietly – d'yer know, I felt happy? –
an' let him out.

BOB. Rose yoo scare me. Ont talk like that, ont even think it.
Yoo're one of us now, yoo hev to think like white folk. We
ont hev madmen with whips – 'less we step out a line an'
meddle: *then* they goo mad! From now on yoo be guided by
me.

ROSE. Take orders? No. I 'ave to take them from them, but
not from you.

BOB (*quietly*). Ont row. Yoo ont understand yoo'll hev to
accept an' thass that. Yoo're a soft gal Rose, too easy
touched: thass a canker.

ROSE. I can be as hard as you. But I won't do the things I
grew up to hate.

BOB (*holds her*). Wish I ont married if thass only gooin' to
bring this sort of trouble. O Rose, Rose . . .

   PARSON *comes in.*

BOB (*holding* ROSE). Beg pardon parson, wife's upset . . .
He's gone.

PARSON. Dear me.

BOB. Ont set the bolt proper. Shook loose. My fault. (*Steps
away from* ROSE.)

PARSON. Bob you cost your master dear. Get after him. Take
every horse and man from the fields. I accept responsi-
bility. We have taken a viper to our bosom. A stranger who
does not love our ways. Pray he has led none of our flock
astray! Thank heavens there are hours of daylight before
us. Scour every road. (*To* MOTHER *as she comes in.*) Did I
spy my glass of madeira under its friendly blue saucer? If
you would be so kind. The excitement has parched my
throat. Bob take my horse too.

BOB. He took the rest of the silver.

MOTHER (*stares*). O the wicked man! (*Bursts into tears.*) My silver gone! I polished it for years! The wicked man! Wicked! (*She weeps and sobs the word 'wicked' as she collects the silver from the floor.*)

PARSON. There: see how the guilty afflict the innocent. This woman learns of a lifetime's wasted labour. The cherished things on which she lavished her affection are gone. How will she occupy the time she would have devoted to cleaning them? I cannot lend her a consoling book, she cannot read. And who is to say that in the hotness of pursuit fear has not triumphed over greed? Even now the loot may lie in the mud at the bottom of a ditch.

MOTHER (*weeping*). O parson don't say so!

PARSON. Or be hurled down a well, lost forever!

MOTHER. Whatever shall us do?

BOB. I'll take the men right out to Coppins Point. He'll hev made for the coach road.

PARSON. Ten commandments! That's all that are asked of us. One little law for each finger, to bring peace to the lord in his palace and the goodman in his cottage. Yet ten are too many. They live by one: self – and seek perdition. Are you confirmed my dear?

ROSE. Yes.

PARSON. A pity. O I rejoice in your salvation. But the darkness of this day would have been lightened by the conversion of a heathen in my own parish. O you mustn't think all Englishmen are rogues my dear. I assure you most are as upright and sensible as your dear husband. Well, I'll fetch the madeira. (*He goes.*)

Man Groans (ROSE *and* MOTHER)

The house is on fire
Dark figures wave from the roof!

Shall we fetch a ladder
Or light brands to burn down the rest of the street?

> You to whom the answer is easy
> Do not live in our time
> You have not visited our city
> You weep before you know who to pity
> Here a good deed may be a crime
> And a wrong be right
> To you who go in darkness we say
> It's not easy to know the light

A man sits hunched in a cell
People dance in the street
Shall we stretch our hands through the bars
Or run to the street and dance in triumph?

> You to whom etc.

A man groans in a ditch
We take off our coat
To cover the man in the ditch or give to the man who runs
    away?

> You to whom etc.

Scene Five

Hilgay.
The Hall.
Breakfast Room.
Table set for breakfast. Two chairs.
ARE *reads a London newspaper.*

ARE. When I go to the city of light Hedges stays here in outer
    darkness. Because my forebears had the lice combed from
    their beards by yokels must I have my cravat ruined by

one? I shall – (*Stops short at what he reads in the paper.* ANN *comes in as a ghost.*) That damned little Lordling Lester! The ninth time he's squirted into print since my departure! Plague rot his little ermined soul! I'll rout that martinet at his capers and see –

He sees the ghost.

Why I'll put on last year's breeches! The family ghost! (*Puts down the paper.*) Mother I beg your pardon. I thought 'twas the gin when it grinned at ye through the windows.

ANN. Woe!

ARE. Be off with ye! Disturbin' a gentleman at his breakfast! (*Picks up his newspaper and shoos it.*) Shoo I say!

ANN. Hear me Lord Are!

ARE. Hear ye? What listen to an ague-ridden corpse! When I want news or advice I'll go to someone a damned sight livelier than thou art ma'am. When were you at court or the play? Ye gad! what d'ye know of fashion? I'll wear something a sight more sprightly to be buried in! It amazeth me ye are not ashamed to be seen so in modern times!

ANN. Thy poor wife!

ARE. My wife? What of my wife? (*Aside.*) Here's a to-do, discussin' me wife with a ghost – though the subject is fitting. Have ye come to tell me she's to join ye? I thank ye for the good news and bid ye be gone so I may celebrate in peace!

ANN (*aside*). The monster! – Thy wife must flee to London. Flee!

ARE. To London? Why?

ANN. She is with child. If 'tis born here 'tis forever cursed.

ARE. Forsooth? And who will bear the expense of a London lying in? Let the cow doctor child her, as he did all my family. A curse? Lawd 'twill curse me for cursing it with its mother! But 'tis to be hoped it's a sensible brat and will understand it was the she-cat or poverty – and his poor papa made the best of the bad bargain.

ANN (*aside*). O my London revenge! I'll smear the paint on his face in the royal presence! – Alas that noble woman!

ARE. If ye pity her go and keep her company. I am not so hard put that I must seek the society of a ghost. I tell ye this spirit: I had thought to have been too harsh with the slut, but if it's with brat I'm off tomorrow. Her morning sickness will be nauseous.

ANN (*aside*). I'll frighten the monster to death!

ANN *goes*.

ARE (*muttering to himself as he settles at the table and resumes his newspaper*). Damned impertinent she-spirit, to disturb a man outside calling hours. I see the editorial doth not advise us the ghosts are walking. 'Tis a good story – yet I cannot use it. I'd have the methodists roaring hymns at my door and asking to see my spirit. Still, the news gives a man relish to his breakfast. London! Blessed city! Our new Jerusalem! Soon my shadow shall fall on thy doorways, my sprightly foot ascend thy broad stairs, my melodious voice sound in thy tapestried halls. London London London thou art all! I thank thee spirit and shall drink thy health when I come to town.

ANN *comes in*.

ANN. Woe! Woe!

ARE. 'Tis intolerable! Have ye come to tell me the news was mistaken?

ANN. Thy poor wife. That dearest, loveliest creature, that paragon of –

ARE. Pox! If thy news is so great it brings thee from the grave twice then tell it!

ANN. If thy wife goes not to London thy wealth is lost!

ARE. This is arrant posturing! She hath raised thee to badger me. She stays. Go! I defy thee. (*Aside.*) 'Fore god I am taken with my style. Who'd have thought I'd unloose such a show of bravado?

ANN. Thy wife –

ARE. Stays.

ANN. Then curses on your ugly face! Your evil old –

ARE. I shall not have my face insulted at breakfast by a zombie!

> ARE *goes.*

ANN. O the wretch! I'll poison him! No I'll poison myself and haunt him!

> ARE *comes back with a drawn rapier.*

ARE. Out vapour! (*Whirls his rapier.*) I shall stir you up and blow you off in a mist!

ANN. O wretch!

ARE. It backs! What – ye remember cold steel? Have at ye! I would not be inhospitable to anyone but ye have a place: the wall – or anywhere at all of Lord Lester's. A man may breakfast at peace in his home before he's reminded there is religion – or it's not England!

> ARE *runs* ANN *through.*

ANN. O. (*Falls.*)

ARE. Why 'tis a heavy ghost! I had thought to go whisk-whisk and – as I am a gentleman – opened the window for it and it had vanished in a puff of smoke. The ghost bleeds. (*Stoops, examines.*) 'Fore god 'tis flesh and blood. My wife. (*Steps back. His voice falls and he presses the index finger to the side of his mouth.*) Hsssssssssssssss ... here's a fine how-d'ye-do. My wife. Stretched out on the floor. With a hole in her breast. Before breakfast. How is a man to put a good face on that? An amendment is called for. It were a foolish figure I should cut. A buffoon. Murdered his wife. Got up like a ghost. Before breakfast. I break into cold sweat when I think of how I should use it had it befallen Lord Lester. I could not put my foot in a duke's door again. Never ascend the stairs to a hall blazing with chandeliers. Or ogle the ladies from the *balcon réservé* of a pump room. My life would be over. (*Nibbles toast.*) Cold. Faw! (*Puts toast down.*) A fine kettle of fish! (*Rings.*) Well you'd best sit at your husband's table. Hopefully 'twill look as if our quarrel had been less violent. Stretched out on the floor can only encourage the lowest surmises. (*Sets* ANN *in a chair.*) A man cannot think with his dead wife sprawled on the carpet. And I must think – after I've tired my brains with choosing a suit for the day.

BOB *comes in.*

ARE. Toast. This is as cold as a corpse – yea, and as hard as a tombstone.
BOB. That be all my lord?
ARE. For the moment.
BOB. Right my lord.

BOB *takes the toast rack from the table and goes.*

ARE. O thou Great Boob. Thou art my deliverer. Thou mayest be relied on. I do not see it yet, but thou art a loon and shall serve. (*Adjusts* ANN.) To arrange thee better. Faith thy silence is wonderful! Hadst thou behaved so when thou livst thou mightst have lived longer. Thy costume becomes thee. At last thy tailor hath done thee justice. Thy face had always a lowering look. You played death to the life. A performance to retire on.

> ARE *goes.* BOB *comes in with toast in a silver rack, goes to the table and steals a cup of coffee. He sees* ANN. *He drops the toast.*

BOB. Eek! Lawd defend us! The dead are risen!

> ARE *comes back.*

ARE. What man?

BOB (*points*). Th – th – th –

ARE. Ye have burned the toast? Twice in one morning!

BOB. No' – th' – no' – th' –

ARE. Is the child possessed?

BOB. Th' – *there*!

ARE (*goes to the chair and looks at* ANN). There is a ghost. O Robert thou art possessed! What have ye done?

BOB. Eek! A ghost!

ARE. How it spies at thee. It comes for thee Robert.

BOB (*sinks to his knees*). O no am I goin' to die? O lawd defend us!

ARE. What venom! Shut thine eyes Bob lest it ensnare thee.

BOB (*shuts his eyes*). Ah! Eek! Oo!

ARE. Take the rapier.

BOB. The –?

ARE. Beside thee. (ARE *kicks the rapier along the floor.*) Hold the handle as a cross.

BOB. Lawd! Lawd! (*One arm across his eyes, the rapier held out in the other hand.*) Mercy! Save us!

> ARE *lifts* ANN *from behind.*

ARE. Robert! Robert! Take care! It advanceth at thee!

BOB (*peeps from under his arm*). Ah! O!

> ARE *manipulates* ANN.

ARE. I struggle with it. It tears itself towards thee. God what strength! It will have ye!

BOB. No! No! No! No!

Terror! ARE *makes ghost sounds and lifts* ANN *towards* BOB. BOB *points the rapier.* ARE *leans* ANN *on the rapier's point.*

ARE. O Robert. Open your eyes.

BOB (*eyes covered*). Hev it gone? (*Uncovers eyes.*)

ARE. See! the ghost – the rapier – you: joined. Bob what have ye done? (*He pushes* ANN *with a finger: she topples.*) Murdered your mistress.

BOB. My mistress?

ARE. 'Tis – 'twas – she. I cannot say why she is so dressed. I do not recall she mentioned a fancy-dress breakfast. It seems unlikely. Who can fathom the mind of one suddenly raised to the peerage? Did she suppose society breakfasted in this extravagant fashion? We can never know. Impetuous Bob, how often have I warned ye?

BOB. Impetuous?

ARE. Certainly. Ye have murdered your mistress. What greater proof of impetuosity?

BOB. But I – took it for a ghost!

ARE. As I say: impetuous Bob. I struggled with ye, but thou art a robust fellow and overcame me – and then, I had not breakfasted.

BOB. What have I done?

ARE. Murdered your mistress. Before breakfast. Pray do not stand there with your rapier dripping blood on my carpet. Hand it to me (*Takes the rapier.*) lest ye turn it against me –

BOB. Never my lord!

ARE. – in your present rashness. In one of your sudden fits. I see it now. A practical joke, a jape. Her ladyship ennuied by rural life – which must be said in her favour – tried thus to brighten our morning. But Bob you have no sense of humour.

BOB. No sir. I just do my job.

ARE. This morning you were overzealous. Well 'twas a paltry accident. Pick up the toast.

BOB (*picking up the toast*). What's to be done sir?

ARE. The future rests with the authorities – as it always does. (*Looks at a piece of toast.*) Blood. I shall not breakfast this morning. Forget the toast. One shudders at what you would do on your third attempt to bring it.

BOB. I begin to see what I hev done: I hev widowed my master.

ARE. Before breakfast. Few can say as much. I shall miss her pranks – this is presumably the last. Bob was I ever a bad master?

BOB. Thass what make it worse! Her poor ladyship.

ARE. Well she was not altogether without blame. Never play jokes on the servants. It agitates them into dropping things. That at least we have learned this morning. (*Rings.*)

BOB. What yoo dooin'?

ARE. We have a difficult road ahead. Turn to me at all times. I shall lead ye to the promised land. Hold no conference with others, who will mislead you.

BOB. Yes sir. I've made my mistake once. O thank yoo sir.

ARE. Do not fumble my hand Bob. Ye have slain my wife and I have completed my toilet.

MOTHER *comes to the door.*

ARE. Mrs Hedges her ladyship is dead.

MOTHER. Beg pardin' sir?

ARE. Her ladyship is dead.

MOTHER. Dead?

ARE (*aside*). O the tedium of a tragedy: everything is said twice and then thrice.

MOTHER (*flatly*): Dead?

ARE (*aside*). Twice.

MOTHER (*flatly*): Dead!

BOB. Dead!

ARE (*aside*). I have survived the morning tolerably well, now I shall spoil it with a headache.

MOTHER (*suddenly realising*). Her ladyship is dead!

ARE (*aside*). If she is not she is a consummate actress.

MOTHER. Is her ladyship dead?

ARE (*aside*). O god is it to be put to the question? We shall have pamphlets issued on it. There are really no grounds for this aspersion on my swordsmanship.

MOTHER. Ah! Er! O! (*Weeps.*)

ARE (*aside*). Now the wailing and hallooing. Lungs of leather from coursing their dogs, throats like organ pipes from roaring their hymns. Well I have an immaculate excuse for retiring to my room, and as it cannot return I shall use it. – Mrs Hedges if ye have no pan on the fire pray run to the magistrate and tell him Bob has murdered his mistress.

MOTHER. Eek! Murdered? Bob?

BOB. Alas!

ARE (*aside*). And now the convulsions they learn at country dancing. – Mind, not parson Mrs Hedges. Captain Sludge. I could not endure parson's consolations on an empty stomach. (Bob throw the toast to the hens on your way to prison.) (BOB, *weeping, picks up the toast rack and nods.*) I shall have to contend with parson at the graveside. Sludge is a plain bluff man who made many fields sanguinary with the blood of his sovereign's foes. He won't set the windows rattling at the sight of one dead woman. Mrs Hedges to Captain Sludge.

BOB. Ought to give her ladyship a sheet. Ont decent lyin' there.

BOB *and* MOTHER *wail.*

Captain's is too far for mother in her state of aggravation. I'll hand meself in.

ARE. 'Tis handsome Bob, but I cannot let a murderer wander the fields. Superstition is rife: the hands would refuse to harvest. – Mrs Hedges the chimney tops will rattle down scattering fire and ash as if Hilgay were the sister city to Gomorrah. Your wailing will start the dogs, the dogs will start the cows, the cows will start the farm and so the next farm and the news of my wife's death will reach London by neighing and mooing. I would have it arrive by a more conventional conveyance. Bob wait. I'll send a man from the kennels. The dogs have been walked.

ARE *goes*.

BOB. If it weren't for his lordship I'd kill meself.

MOTHER. Don't talk so daft. (*She hits him*.) Put a brave face on it. Parson'll speak up for yoo if his lordship doo. Whole a Hilgay'll rally round. Yoo ont step out a line before – not till yoo married. An yoo married her in London (*She hits him*.) so it ont count. Why! if they had to find an ordinary chap they ont find one more ordinary than yoo boy.

Part Two

Scene Six

Peterborough.
Gaol.
Cell. Upstage door to another cell. ROSE *and* BOB. BOB *is shackled to the floor.*

ROSE. What happened?

BOB. She were in the chair. Dress up like a ghost. O I on't know.

ROSE. Let me help you.

BOB. Can't help. It'll be all right. (*He tries to comfort her but she walks away.*)

ROSE. Show me what happened.

BOB. (*half demonstrates*). I goo to the table. Toast. Hev a look. She's sat there. Hands like so. Blood. (*Puts finger on chest. Keeps it there.*) Yell. Lordship run in. Took howd of sword –

ROSE. How did she move?

BOB Horrible. He tries to howd her. She howl. Stick sword out. Open me eyes. (*Uncovers his face.*) Sword in her. (*Puts a finger on the place where the sword went in.*) Topples down dead.

ROSE. Yer said the blood was here. (*Points at the higher finger.*)

BOB (*looks at the two fingers – one on his chest, the other on his stomach*). Ont know. (*Shakes his head.*) 'S'n accident.

ROSE. They have accidents, we make mistakes.

ARE, PARSON *and* GAOLER *come in.*

ARE. Robert you bear up bravely.

BOB. Sir. Parson.

PARSON. Bless you. (*To* ROSE.) Bless you child.

ARE (*aside* to PARSON). This is a sorry sight: my livery in a cell. Cannot ye find him suitable clothes in the charity bundle?

> ARE *tips the* GAOLER. *He goes.*

PARSON. My lord. My sister shall attend to it.

BOB. We're jist tryin' to sort out what happened.

ARE. Bob Bob, why trouble your head with things that don't concern it? If I can't manage the affair as I see fit I may have to withdraw.

BOB. Ont do that sir.

ARE. I cannot be made a public lampoon. The good shepherd who found his sheep and lost it on the way home.

ROSE. Her ladyship was sitting in –

ARE. Like a loyal wife your head is in as great a whirl as your husband's. (*Aside.*) The turnkey shall forbid her the cell. 'Tis seemly in a hanging.

ROSE (*to* PARSON). Her ladyship was sitting in the chair bleeding.

ARE. Bleeding? (*Aside.*) I repeat myself like the rest.

FRANK. (*off*). Pleasure brought me to my end! What brought you, yer cantin' hypocrite?

ARE (*to* PARSON). My former footman. When we're finished here I'll go and rattle my cane through his bars.

BOB (*calls*). Ont hang. His lordship stand by me.

FRANK (*off*). Trust that fox an' yer deserve t' hang! Bang the door in his face! Yer no friend of mine Bob Hedges but I don't wish him on yer!

ARE. Don't heed him Bob. His present position don't qualify him to give advice.

ROSE. So she was bleedin' before Bob stabbed her.

PARSON (*shrugs*). Child the whole thing is beyond human –

ARE. Have ye never took a flower from a vase in the hall and stuck it in your coat as ye left the house? She sprinkled herself with paint on the way down as a final touch.

ROSE. We can see if there's paint on the sheet.

FRANK (*off*). Ask 'em to hang yer to music! Show the girl's yer fancy dancin' kicks!

ROSE. And the sword on the floor? How –

ARE. Mr Phelps next door.

PARSON. My lord?

ARE. We cannot let that fellow die with his soul in such neglect. For charity, go to him.

PARSON. Your lordship is a wonder! Even now I was silently praying I might be asked.

> PARSON *goes out to fetch the* GAOLER.

ARE. Well miss?

ROSE. My husband didn't kill her.

BOB. (*quietly*). Bless you Rose. Yoo're the brave one here.

ARE. Bob –

BOB. She were bleedin' when I come in.

ARE. Let me consider. (*Goes to one side.*) The sun rose on the horizon – and fell back, and all the world is darkness. Courage good heart. If the sun goes from its course, why – bring it back. The oaf will hang and the truth with him. But it must be done quietly, and now the hussy will drag me in. Lester will scrawl me up on the wall of every jakes as a jack-in-the-box with a sword in its hand! 'Tis intolerable.

ROSE (*to* BOB). Does his lordship always eat breakfast with a sword?

ARE (*goes back to them*). Bob I must tell thee plainly thou art a trouble and deserve thy wife: yet I wish ye the same happy deliverance I had. What you or I say is no matter. Truth is what the lawyers say it is. You have none, whilst I . . .

(*Gesture*.) If Bob confesses, the killing is an accident. If he accuses me – well, have ye ever listened dumbfounded while ye contradicted yourself ten times in a minute? My lawyers will torment him till he runs to the scaffold – many an innocent man has willingly hanged to be rid of a lawyer. What if I go into the dock? 'Tis still an accident. But what a fool I must seem! Marrying the coalman's daughter blemished my name, but this – 'tis a scene from a farce. I cannot say why I did not know she was my wife. Had a kinder providence set the scene in a London salon, under two chandeliers, I'd have recognised her even with one of her father's buckets over her head. Would ye give evidence against me Bob. A lord dragged down by a working man? 'Tis against all civil order. Ye see the enormity of the thing? We are at the heart of the matter. In my person I am society, the symbol of authority, the figurehead of law and order. Make me a fool or a villain and the mob will dance in the street. If ye will be innocent, Bob, anarchy must triumph, your windows be broken, your mother's head cracked and your wife stoned for a blackamoor (He *takes* BOB *aside. His chain rattles*.) Come, we are Englishmen and may talk freely together. Ye have this chance to serve your country. Robert the Hero, hail! The nation asks it of ye. Stand trial. Be aquitted. I'll buy the jury. I withdraw while ye consider your reply.

The Gentleman (BOB *and* ROSE)
He steps out of the way to let her pass
On one arm she carries a child
In the other a battered case
With the hinges broken
Tied with a strap
He takes the child and holds it on his shoulder
He opens the gate to let the woman pass

He has not seen her till now
What politeness he shows the stranger!
In his hand there's a rifle
At the door to the gas chamber
He hands the child back to her arms

> Who would raise a whip when an order is obeyed?
> Why lift up your fist when a pointing finger will lead?
> Who would raise their voice when soft words will do my
> friend?
> Why use a knife when a smile makes cuts that bleed?
> When you have the mind why bother to chop off the
> head?
> When white hands will do the work why make your hands
> red?

> THE PARSON *returns with the* GAOLER. *The* GAOLER
> *lets the* PARSON *into the cell upstage. The* GAOLER
> *lounges beside the open door and waits.*

ROSE. The judge is staying at the Tabard. I'll go into –
BOB. Wait, we can't afford to make an enemy of him.
ROSE. He is our enemy. He's guilty and you're innocent.
BOB. Yes, but that ont seem to matter. We accuse him we'll
   starve gal. Never git another job's long's we live. We jist
   hev to go along for the sake of appearance – like he say.
ROSE. Yer said yer always obey the law.
BOB. But he is the law – so I must obey him.
ROSE. But he's guilty and you're –
BOB (*head in hands*). Ont know what I ought t' do! Less think
   woman!
FRANK (*off*). Sold the silver and lived like a lord. Whored in
   the mornin', whored in the afternoon, whored in the eve-
   nin' when I weren't pissed!
ARE (*calls*). Confound it parson, pray to some effect!

FRANK (*off*). He's on his knees doin' his best, aren't yer old cock?

THE PARSON *comes in.*

PARSON. Patience sir. When they're to hang there's nothing to threaten them with. Not even hell. In this atheistical age they don't believe in it.

THE PARSON *goes back into the cell*

FRANK (*off*). Swillin' and screwin' till the landlord stopped me. He had one eye: I watched it swivel. Bastard knew me silver was runnin' out, just waitin' till the reward was bigger than what I had left. Slipped off in time. Lived in the fields. Robbed the churches.

PARSON (*off*). 'Tis not a confession, 'tis boasting.

FRANK (*off*). Jumped out the hedges onto the women and screwed 'em in the ditch! The last wild beast in England! I almost made London!

ARE (*to* ROSE). By the by, I brought the rapier in for Bob to polish.

FRANK (*off*). Open winder in Barnet. Put me hand in. Son of the house crep' up behind. Knock me out. Thick country lout. Drag back here. But it was worth it!

ARE (*calls*). Parson muzzle him with your cassock. – Robert my business presses.

BOB. A minute longer.

FRANK (*off*). Oi! is that Lord Arse?

PARSON (*off*). Purge his heart and still his tongue.

PARSON *runs out of the cell.* GAOLER *slams the door and locks it.*

FRANK. (*appears at the grill in the door*). Is that you Arsehole?

BOB (*to* ROSE): Least this way we got a chance.

ROSE. I won't keep quiet.

FRANK (*at grill*). Arsehole! I can smell yer! I thought it was the prison sewer! God rot yer, yer'll hang one day yer bastard! Yer pox ridden rat!

BOB (*to* ROSE): I've said I did it, said sorry! They'd laugh in me face if I towd the truth now –

ROSE. If we don't it'll be too late.

FRANK (*at grill*). Arsehole!

ARE (*rattling his cane through the grill*). Fellow if your insults had any wit I'd stay to applaud. (*To* BOB:) Tis a great sadness but I see ye will stand on your own.

> ARE *goes to the door and is about to leave.* BOB *gestures to him to wait.*

FRANK (*at grill*). Arsehole! I thought my life had no more pleasure! It's worth hanging to call you cur to your face! I watched you lie in your vomit! Fool! I deserve to hang for not throttling you then!

BOB. It's according as your lordship wishes.

ARE. Good – you choose your protector well.

FRANK (*falls down*). Rot yer!

> *Sounds of raving.* GAOLER *opens the door of* FRANK's *cell.* PARSON *goes in and almost immediately comes out to shout at* ARE.

PARSON. Beware! Your lordship's adjacency brings on convulsions. He crawls upon his stomach on the floor. He'll die before scaffolding day!

> ARE *goes.*

BOB (*to* ROSE): I played the sheep, now I'll play the man. I'll git us through. Ont fret Rose. I'd rather hev yoor smile.

PARSON (*peers through the open door of the cell at* FRANK). A serpent or a great newt!

FRANK (*off*). Rot! Rot! Rot him!

PARSON (*running down stage*). Gaoler! Tis from Revelations!

FRANK *lurches into the cell. His hands are manacled. His leg chain pulls him short and he crashes to the floor.*

Song of Talking (BOB *and* FRANK)

My mate was a hard case
Worked beside me on the bench for years
Hardly said a word
Talking isn't easy
When the machines run
One day he dropped a coin
He unscrewed the safety rail to get it back
The press-hammer struck his head
He looked up at the roof and he said
　The green hills by the sea
　Where the light shines
　Through tall dark pines
A minute later he was dead

Didn't speak even on the street
Once I saw him shopping with his wife
He only nodded
He was decent to me
But I'd heard rumours
He'd done time in chokey
And his fist could hit you like a steel-capped boot
Then he unscrewed the safety-rail
I nursed him on the concrete floor
He looked up at the roof and said
　The green hills by the sea
　In the dark grove
　I first made love
A minute later he was dead

You didn't pick a row with him
Once I bumped him on the parking lot

No real damage
He stared through his windscreen
Then drove off fast
A frown made him handsome
I never knew what team he supported
Then he unscrewed the safety-rail
I nursed him on the concrete floor
He looked up at the roof and said
    The green hills by the sea
    Where the gulls cry
    In the white sky
A minute later he was dead

My mates ran to fetch the nurse
The foreman wouldn't stop the machines
I bent to listen
He looked like an apprentice
He was gently crying
And babbling to himself
I touched his hand – no response
The hammer was still beating
I nursed him on the concrete floor
He looked up at the roof and said
    The green hills by the sea
    Through the tall dark trees
    The sea weaves
    A shining thread
A minute later he was dead

Scene Seven

Hilgay.
Copse.
Off, from time to time pig bells and pig grunts.
ROSE *and* GABRIEL, *the blind swineherd.*

ROSE. They found him guilty.

GABRIEL. He'll hang. Never seen my boy's face.

ROSE. Are killed her. Bob's covering up.

GABRIEL. Hev he any witness?

ROSE. No.

GABRIEL. Then best howd yoor row ... People allus fuss
over what they can't mend. The whole world tip up
an' everyone slid off – thass jist a saucer of spilt milk. Tell
yoo what: know a sow's carryin' be the way her bell
waddle. Another hev a great fat sound, thass time for the
butcher. This job's all Sundays, like sit listenin' to bacon
in the pan. Wife, roof, dry sty, eat an' sleep like an old
boar.

ROSE. You talk Gabriel. Yer'd see if yer could. Even if it were
jist ten minutes an' yer had to watch Bobby hang.

GABRIEL. Wrong gal. Ont hev it, ont want it. Sight's a curse
laid on them who lead me, feed me, thatch the roof an'
hang the door – life a sweat an' grind an' small pittance in
the end. Better off sat in the sun, an' in the copse when it's
hot. Ont bother no one. Break me cane, I git home feelin'
'long the trees. Whass the use of talkin' to neighbours? –
could be winkin' in me face all I know. Got blind fightin' in
France. Ont see the chap that took my sight – lookin' the
other way at the time. After, they're all rejoicin' 'cause we
won the war, an' I say: now what, can't work like this? –
end up on street corner collectin' rain in me hat. Happen
lucky, the old swineherd took it in his head to die an' I got

took on at his job. Now where's the chap that hit me?
Could a bin dead next day, fell off a ship, tree struck him.
Who's to say what luck is? I hev the fruit of the world
without its pains. Bar one. Mornin's – jist afore I wake –
dream I hev me sight. Run up the hill, wave me arms an'
holler at the sun. Then I wake up an' say: thass jist the boy
left over in me. So I ont sneer at it – an' I ont weep. Yoo see
before yoo a happy man.

MOTHER *comes in.*

GABRIEL. What yoo all hot an' cross for mother?

MOTHER. She ont supposed to interfere with yoor work.
Lose a pig there's all hell to pay. Whass she bin sayin'?

GABRIEL. Nothin'.

MOTHER. Hardache's up at the cottage. Push the door open
with his stick an' say yoo wrote him. Sent him round the
long way an' cut cross the fields. You let on whass gooin' on
here, I'll cuss the day you wed my boy.

ROSE. He'll help Bob.

MOTHER. Ont need help.

ROSE. They'll hang him.

MOTHER. Ont talk such rot. No sense of proportion. This
is his big chance. Doo his lordship a favour like this an' he's
set up for life. Poor people can't afford to waste a chance
like this, god know it ont come often. Time our luck
change. Yoo start trouble, who pay? Us. Yoo're off to
London, we git chuck out. End up at the workhouse.
Work like a slave, workhouse disease – ont last six months,
seen it afore. Too old to hev my life mess up. Look at him:
come back from France an' got took on 's if he had twenty
eyes. Could a cost his lordship no end of pig. He stood by
him – like he doo Bob. So ont meddle Rose.

ROSE. We can't risk it. Bob's in prison waitin' to –

MOTHER. Worse places outside. Ont expect his lordship to

goo in the dock for the like of her. Jist drag his family name through the mire. Whatever next! Ont know where to look next time I went to the village, they knew I work for someone like that. 'S'n accident *who* it was. Silly woman deserve to git killed. She come into my kitchen dress' up I give her a whack of my fryin' pan she ont git up from.

ROSE. He's hanged but the roof's over yer head.

MOTHER. You think I'm that sort of woman, my dear, thass yoor privilege.

ROSE. O I don't understand you people!

MOTHER. Jist ont stand in my boy's way when he hev his chānce to goo up in the world. Lie on oath doo it help him, say I saw him run to fetch the sword.

ROSE. Why should Arseface help him? Bob's a labourer, no better than –

GABRIEL. Howd both yoor rows, yoo upset my pigs. The same thing if he kill her or not. (*Calls.*) Sibby! – If thass between him an' his boss, stand to reason who win. Drat pig! After them acorns at Pallin's End.

ROSE. It's not between Are and Bob. It's between two bosses.

MOTHER. Now whass she on about?

ROSE. When yer black, it pays t'know the law. No one can benefit from their own crime. Are killed his wife – so he loses her money. It goes back to the next of kin: her father.

HARDACHE *comes in. He fans his face, neck and inside his jacket with his hat.*

HARDACHE. Pretty place. Sorry I had to miss the funeral. A neighbour had to sell up and I couldn't miss the opportunity. Then the trial: had to arrange a little shares shenanigans. Rose, you married a villain but no one's perfect. All the bitterness was squeezed out of me long ago when my first warehouse went up on fire. Tell Bob I haven't wept since.

MOTHER. It was accidental Mr Hardache.

HARDACHE. Ay lass, but some have accidents and some don't. Lads keep falling into my furnaces all the time. You'd think they did it on purpose. I see a furnace I go round it not in it. And if I saw a ghost I'd leave the room like any sensible man – unless it were me late wife.

MOTHER. That wicked gal's got it into her head my Bob didn't do it.

HARDACHE. Not do it? Is that right Rose? Then who did?

ROSE. Are.

HARDACHE. His lordship. Nay I've never heard the like. Happy young couple like that? Why ever should he be so rash? No, she were struck down by your overhasty young man. I can't believe otherwise. His lordship you say?

MOTHER. Yoo talk sense into her sir.

HARDACHE. Well I'm struck both ways sideways. What a predicament to fall into our laps – (*quickly correcting himself*) land on our heads. A real taramadiddle and no mistake. Did he strike her Rose?

ROSE. Yes sir and talked Bob into taking the blame.

HARDACHE. I shan't take kindly to bein' deceived Mrs Hedges. Now's the time to speak out. You know what's at stake: my daughter's memory. D'you know owt?

MOTHER. Well – I doo an' I don't. What should I say?

HARDACHE. The truth woman! It's a christian country, i'n't it?

MOTHER. Well – if his lordship kill her – what's the good of what I say?

HARDACHE. What good? Does justice count for nothing in these parts? When I think of that innocent young man – you did say he was innocent, Rose? – alone in his cell, my withers weren't more wrung for me own daughter. Well Mrs Hedges?

MOTHER. I suppose – if thass how it is – I hev to tell Mr Hardache that my son towd me he ont do it.

HARDACHE. And also testified that Are cajoled him into covering up his own crime. What a dastardly villain!

MOTHER (*finishing repeating his words*). . . . his own crime what a dastardly villain.

HARDACHE. Well. Now we know. I'm right glad I came to pay respects to my daughter's grave: you run into business anywhere.

ROSE. Mr Hardache you're our only friend.

HARDACHE. And you'll never have a better. Leave all to me lass. Mind, no speakin' out of turn. The fish still has to be landed by an expert tickler. Good day.

ROSE. Will yer go straight to the judges?

HARDACHE. Tch tch didn't I say leave all to me?

ROSE. I'll show you the quick way to the house.

> HARDACHE *and* ROSE *go.*

GABRIEL. If yoo was indoors the roof'd fall on yoor head.

MOTHER. Caught me between.

GABRIEL (*calls*). Sibby! Yoo git fat yoo jist make work for the butcher. – Gad woman them pigs talk more sense'n yoo.

Legend of Good Fortune (MOTHER)

Men lived in peace and plenty
When the world was as young as the day
But a god came down from heaven
And took the good things away

He put them all in a basket
And slowly climbed up to his cave
He put the basket under his head
And slept like a weary slave

There passed on earth ten ages of war
Men groaned and lived as the dead
When the dreaming god stirred in his sleep
And the basket fell out of his bed

Then from the heavens there rained on man
The gifts of plenty and peace
Bread and honey and fruit and wine
And the new golden age began

Slowly the god woke up from his sleep
And came down to rob again
This time men said what we have we shall keep!
And they fought till the god was slain

Send for the wise to share your bread
Take the beautiful into your bed
And if ever that god is seen in your land
Take all he's got – and break his head!

Scene Eight

Peterborough.
Holme Cottage.
Table. Chairs.
BOB *and* PARSON.
BOB'*s legs are fettered. He scratches a pen on paper.*

BOB. I hev a skill for learnin', jist lacked the opportunity
afore. Hev terrible difficulty with my S. Squiggly ijit of a
letter. Letters is a miracle! Dance afore yoor eyes an'
suddenly goo t'gither like a candle flarin' up an' a chap see
all he look at. Are say I'll be put in charge of clerkin'.

Scribe letters an' bills. Chap born in a cottage ont hope to rise so high.

PARSON. Bob, hope for a pardon, yes. But it may not come. Hope for salvation.

BOB. Parson ont yoo be so glum. For the moment us hev to make the best of a bad way. Our pardon'll come an' if it ont, why, they hang me with Frank, he's such a sharp thief he'll steal the rope an' we'll both git off. There that ont a bad joke for a chap in my plight! Come now, old friend, ont like to see yoo so depress'. Cheer up an' smile.

PARSON. You are under sentence of death. Try to reap some benefit from that. Surely god is teaching you a lesson greater than any I may?

BOB. 'S natural yoo fret, I understand how yoo feel: but it ont help. Now yoo look on the bright side, or I'll git cross.

PARSON (*aside*). The child is a simpleton. Lord Are promises a pardon to comfort him, but heaps coals of fire on his head. – Bob, pretend – nay pretend, I say – thou dost not get thy pardon. Imagine it for the good of thy soul.

BOB. Can't imagine. Ont interrupt a chap. I'll hev my letters so I can read my pardon. Imagine *that*.

PARSON (*aside*). Well, let us leave him to his book. If he go to heaven with a mind able to read he will show God he hath laboured to put some light into its natural darkness.

BOB. M-a-n-i-s-w-h-a-t-weehat –

PARSON. What.

BOB. H-e-k-n-o-w-s-kernose.

PARSON. Knows.

BOB. Ask me, the chap who invented spellin' ont know how to write. Yoo high-ups ought to sort it out.

MRS WILSON *comes in.*

WILSON. Don't splash your ink on my ceiling. Your mother's here. Look at the mess on my floor.

BOB. Drag in the mud when I pumped water in the yard.

WILSON. You could have wiped them when you wiped your feet.

> MRS WILSON *takes a duster from her pocket.* BOB *cleans his fetters with it.* MRS WILSON *goes out.*

PARSON. Long ago a man called Socrates – a pagan but without other spot – was sentenced to be put to death by poison, after the manner of those days. Now that wise man did not seek pardon. Saying 'He who loves wisdom obeys his country's laws with a gladsome heart' he drank his cup to the lees. We should learn from that wise pagan.

BOB (*dusting*). Was he a writin' man?

PARSON. His words were written down.

BOB. I'll look him up when I git home.

PARSON (*sighs*). The Bible will meet thy needs. (MRS WILSON *comes in and sweeps the floor round* BOB *and the* PARSON.) God spake the word and there was light. Man and woman to cleave unto him. And the birds and beasts of that ineffable garden. The stars in the firmament and the greater and lesser lights –

BOB (*throws the duster down*). Done.

PARSON. – and the waters that roll on the bed of the sea. And the law of life. Look therefore that ye speak and teach wisely: for man is what he knows.

> MOTHER *comes in.*

BOB. Mother. Bear up old gal.

MOTHER. Bob.

> *They don't embrace because she must put down her shopping.*

WILSON. Kettle's on.

MRS WILSON *goes out.*

BOB. Where's Rose?

MOTHER. Ont allowed in.

BOB. Why not?

MOTHER. Ont make the law.

BOB (*to* PARSON). Why not?

PARSON. Perhaps a regulation.

MOTHER. She's outside. (*Shrugs.*) Would come.

BOB (*goes to the door. Calls*). Rose! Rose!

PARSON. I'll go to her. Remember your promise: the best behaviour.

BOB. I want her here!

PARSON *goes.*

MOTHER. Well if thass all the welcome I git I'll goo home. Thought it'd blow over by now. Hev yoo back at yoor job.

Knocking on the ceiling.

BOB. Sod.

BOB *goes.* MOTHER *looks round in bewilderment and fatigue.* MRS WILSON *comes in with the tea things.*

WILSON. Where's Bob.

MOTHER (*looks at ceiling. Vaguely*). Knockin'.

WILSON. Mr Wilson, my husband. Sit down. You look worn out. (*Lays the table.*) I make him wash and brush his hair. Some of them lose interest towards the end. No trouble with his appetite. I can't begrudge what I put on the plate. I'll be out of pocket. I was surprised how little Lord Are was willing to pay. It's so much nicer here than in the cells next door. (*Pours one cup of tea.*) If he gets off (O I'm sure he will) Mr Wilson loses his hanging money. This was supposed to make up the loss – which means it'll add to it.

MOTHER. Thankyoo.

WILSON. Mr Wilson's poorly. They say it's nothing but I know better. Those two are like father and son. Bob's propped his stick by the bed. Soon's he hears the rap he's up those stairs, rattling away. I don't say. D'you eat turf cakes? I made these little ones. There. I'm not the sort of person to count what they put on the plate. Five.

MOTHER. Thankyoo.

WILSON. His turns get worse. Passed the age for outside work. It's a holiday for them, but that's what it is for him.

> BOB *comes in.*

Try not to clank dear. My head's been arguing with me all morning. We're down to three. I don't suppose we'll eat them all. Why didn't you offer your mother a chair, you rude boy? I don't mind who uses them.

> BOB *writes on a corner of the table.*

Mr Wilson says his assistant couldn't take a sweet out of a bag if you opened it first. We daren't give the job up, even I can't manage on what he makes next door. I like to have things round me, otherwise what is there to show? A change of curtains. Proper tea things but that lid's cracked. A carpet upstairs. A few pairs of Sunday gloves. They stick out a mile when everyone puts their hands up to pray. You feel a pauper if you haven't got a change of colour.

MOTHER. Thankyoo.

WILSON. I'll put the tin beside the plate. Then what we don't eat can jump back. Help yourself. (*She pushes the plate further away.*) They ought to bring it indoors. There's always talk but it comes to nothing. Out all weathers. Once the ice was so thick on the rope they had to take turns in breathing on it. Now Mr Wilson ties it under the horse's belly to keep it warm. He's come home with the buttons frozen to his coat. Had a dead cat thrown at him once. No wonder he has turns. And the abuse if they fancy someone! You'd think it was all done for his benefit. I tell him 'They'd know if they let them all off'. He said 'I think they will next'. That was after the cat. Mind, there's two sides isn't there? The better class tip. But you can't even rely on them. One day they might just shake your hand. Even if I know he's got a busy week ahead I can't say 'I'll go out and buy that new teapot'. (*To* BOB.) What was it this time?

BOB (*writing*). Hand shook an' splash his shirt. Had to howd his cup.

WILSON. O don't tell me he's having one of those. Eat your turf cake.

BOB. Ont hungry.

WILSON. O a mood is it?

BOB. No.

WILSON. Don't have moods in my house. We set the cat on them. Well when you ask it'll be gone. (*She eats his cake.*)

Knock on ceiling.

BOB. Drat! Forgot his Bible.

WILSON. What are our young people coming to? Fancy forgetting a Bible! Under that chair. (*Calls.*) Bible's on its way. – You are a funny lad at times. (*To* MOTHER.) It occupies his mind when he's like this. He writes all the births and baptisms and weddings in the front –

BOB *goes out with the Bible.*

– and his work in the back. Glues in extra pages. Goes through them to soothe his mind. Reminds him of all sorts of things he's forgotten. Memory plays funny tricks. I'll clear away, there are light-fingered gentlemen around. I'll wrap that cake with the bite in the side. I believe that was you. It'll do for the way back.

MOTHER (*gently tugs* MRS WILSON'*s sleeve*). His wife's outside. It preys on his mind.

MR HARDACHE *comes in.*

HARDACHE. Mrs Hedges. Ma'am. His lordship's here.

BOB *comes in.*

Say nothing Bob. I can read your face. A harmless prank and you were the engine of fate. Here's half a guinea.

WILSON. Half a guinea.

BOB. Thanks. (*Gives it to* MOTHER.) Rose have that.

WILSON. Mr Hedges you're as thoughtless as my guests next door. Now what have you got for tips?

LORD ARE *and* PARSON *come in.*

ARE. Bob, these are better –

BOB. Rose ont allowed in.

ARE. You'll see her soon.

BOB. Rather see her now. Goo back to the cell if thass necessary.

ARE. Surly Bob, do not abuse my trust.

BOB. Ont hev her stood in the street.

ARE (*aside*). Well, move how he may it only tightens the rope. – Ye make it deuced awkward for your friends Bob. I broke regulations when I took you from your cell as a pledge of your release. Let the blame fall on me again. Fetch her parson. She was on the corner as we passed.

PARSON *goes.*

BOB. Hev yoo my pardon sir? Let me see it.

ARE. I have it not on me, but 'tis safe. There's a style to these things Bob. The terror of the law, majesty of office and so forth. 'Tis not unknown for it to be held back till the man comes to the scaffold. Never lose hope. When you think the hangman is reaching for your neck he may be handing you your pardon.

HARDACHE (*taking* ARE *to one side*). We have a little business to settle.

ARE. What Mr Hardache?

HARDACHE. Your murder of my daughter.

ARE. Bob, show your mother your letters. I'm having him taught his letters Mrs Hedges.

MOTHER. There! I shall hev a readin' an' writin' son. (MOTHER *and* BOB *sit at the table.*)

BOB. I writ Rose. Parson can mix the letters up to spell eros – an' that, he say, is the lower form of love.

ARE (*to* HARDACHE). The Black Slut? – Father-in-law you did not build your empire by listening to trash.

HARDACHE. Wrong lad, I listened to it very well. I call you lad because I notice you've started to call me father. I dont like interfering – but she was my daughter and she'd want the right man to hang.

ARE (*calm and precise*). Why here at such a time?

HARDACHE. Where better? All parties to hand. If questions have to be asked they can answer them directly. And if you have to take lodgings in the prison next door – you're spared the extra journey.

ARE. Sir. My drinking companion the lord lieutenant – in whose bosom my hand lies deeper than ever the dearly beloved disciple's lay in christ's – will not let you clap me into gaol. Tomorrow I am promised for the races, and twould quite spoil his party.

HARDACHE. Son-in-law. Your title gives you acquaintance, money gives me mine. I pay for the coach that takes your mighty friend to the races. Here's a riddle: why does a sensible man like me let his daughter marry a fop like you?

ARE. Fop? A fella don't boast but –

HARDACHE. Coal.

ARE. I misheard.

HARDACHE. No. Under your land.

ARE. I have been rooked.

HARDACHE. Your title cost me a packet but I meant to pay for it with your coal. The marriage made it mine. Or my grandson's – I think ahead for the good of the firm. The firm'ld do very nicely out of thee and me. Now this mishap upsets my grand scheme.

ARE. Why didn't my steward tell me I had coal?

HARDACHE. I paid him not to. But you can't have disloyal retainers round you, lad, so I sacked him on my way here and put my man in his place.

ARE. Father-in-law you are Father Satan.

HARDACHE. Ay well you meant that as flattery but happen when you know me better you'll think it's deserved. (*Document.*) Here's a simple agreement of intent. Our lawyers will work out the details later. All what's over your land is yours: that goes for the late Lady Are's money. What's under is mine: barrin' your ancestors' bones. Sign, and my daughter can sleep in peace for a very long time.

ARE. Bob lend me thy pen.

BOB. Expect a pardon look like that.

HARDACHE. Happen it does for some.

ARE (*signs*). This day I sign an alliance with the devil.

ROSE *comes in.* BOB *embraces her.*

BOB. Ont mind if the people see our joy, all's friends here.

MOTHER. Can't stay long Rose. Miss the cart back.

ROSE. Mr Hardache did you go to the court?

HARDACHE. Lass I considered it but it won't wear.

(ARE *leaves*. MOTHER *collects her things and goes to the door*.) You offer no evidence. Take my advice, keep mum. Bob can show me his pardon when it comes. I'll see he's set up in a good way.

Hurrah! (*All those on stage*)

When Englishmen owned half the world
All Englishmen were brave
And every Englishman was free
And cursed the foreign knave
Who meekly bowed to tyranny
When England ruled the mighty sea
All Englishmen learned at their mother's knee
That England was the home of liberty

Her prisons were houses for the dead
And on her gallows tree
The people hanged for stealing bread
Why steal when you are free?
They let him walk the streets in rags
Or dressed him up in soldier red
And taught him the service of the dead
Hurrah! for every Englishman is free
Old England is the home of liberty

They drove him to the factory like a slave
Or chained him like a beast
To crawl in darkness to his grave
His torments never cease
Till butchered in the wars of kings
His mutilated body sings
Hurrah! for every Englishman is free
Old England is the home of liberty

And so the generations go
Into the fire and into the woe

Into the trenches and into the blood
Bellowing shouts of brotherhood!
They break their brothers' bones when they are told
They think they walk in freedom? – they are sold
To the butcher!
They run to fetch the tackle and hook
They write their names in his invoice book
They whet the blade and hand the knife
They stretch their neck and give their life
Hurrah! for every Englishman is free
Old England is the home of Liberty

HARDACHE. Let's leave the youngsters to their peace.

All go except BOB *and* ROSE.

ROSE. I tried to make him help us. Dog don't eat dog when
they can fight over a bone. I'm going outside, climb on the
wall of the gaol and shout 'Are is a murderer'.
BOB. Rose he promise –
ROSE. He promised they wouldn't find you guilty.
BOB. He explained. Can't buy a whole jury. There was a
Methodist on it. Look, old Lady Are was the king's whore
or summat. Anyroad, she's got the pardon in the bag.
ROSE. Then why ain't you got it?
BOB. Can't jist hand em out. Hev to do things proper
way.
ROSE. I've got money. We could get that chain off –
BOB (*removes leg from fetter*). Thass only for show.
ROSE. God! Then we can go! There's a fast coach to Lynn!
We'll be on the boat tonight!
BOB. Thass madness! I git caught I git hang!
ROSE. You are caught!
BOB. What boat? Where to?
ROSE. Africa! Liberia!

BOB. What I do in the jungle?

ROSE. What I do here!

BOB. 'S different for men. Liberia! That where food grow on trees? Break a stone an' milk come out?

ROSE. Bob the door is open. The window's open. Step through it. If it was shut yer could kick it down. Yer could push the wall down. You're strong. You're a giant. But yer sit and wait to be hanged.

BOB. How I do love thee Rose. All ont lost yet. When I ont git a pardon, then I'll speak out!

ROSE. Too late.

BOB. I am an Englishman, a freeborn Englishman. I hev a right to speak – to shout for all to hear! Thass in our law. Stand up – in court, the street corner, top of the roof – an' shout the truth. It must be so!

ROSE. You're a slave but don't know it. My mother *saw* her chains, she's had marks on her wrists all her life. There are no signs on *you* till you're dead. How can yer fight for freedom when yer think you've got it? What happens to people like you? It's a circus! The clown kicks the mongrel and it licks his boots. He kicks it harder and it rolls on its back an' wags its tail – an' all the dogs laugh. Yer won't go, if there was a chance he'd put yer a mile underground an' chain yer to the wall. Then yer'd be free: yer'd know what you are.

ROSE *goes out.*

BOB. All my life I struggled. Bob the joker. Bob the sport. Walk down the road, the sun shines, eat, work – struggle to keep body and soul together. Yoo got yoor strength, Bob, yoo can do anythin'. Where did I goo wrong? I know well enough. I know what yoo tell me now. Long ago I should hev put my boot in their teeth every time the bastards smiled at me. But I've left it late. Now it's dark. Black.

Black. Black. I must goo steady, or make a terrible blunder. I must trust the clown an' hope for my reward.

Song of the Conjuror (ROSE *and* BOB)

The conjuror tied his hands with an invisible rope
He bound his feet with a chain no one could see
He shut himself in a sack that was not there
And locked it with an invisible key
He hung from a hook over a deep dark lake
The people laughed as he struggled in the air
They stood in crowds to watch him twist and shake
With a fanfare he is free!

The conjuror was the idol of the people
He appeared at every festival in the land
He hung far over the top of every steeple
Turning and twisting and bobbing upside down
He struggled to get the invisible key
The people roared and laughed at his clever tricks
With a fanfare he is free!

One day when he turned in his invisible sack
He could not get free
He screamed like a man stretched on the rack
Which no one could see
His mouth was gagged with invisible rags
More more! roared the crowd and waved their flags
As he writhed in the air
And fought for his life in an unseen snare

They gasped as he fell – the splash
Turned the water white
They screamed as they watched him struggle and thrash
With horror they saw him sinking down
And stood on the bank to watch him drown.

Scene Nine

London.
Old Lady Are's house.
Drawing Room.
ROSE *and* OLD LADY ARE.
OLD LADY ARE *in a chair. On the floor, across the room, a decanter.*

ROSE. They say my husband murdered your daughter-in-law.

LADY ARE. I shall send him a guinea. I never saw the slut. Her father hawked coals in Manchester and she trotted beside him calling his wares. A suitable training for one destined to converse with my son.

ROSE. My husband didn't kill her.

LADY ARE. D'you like fish? It lures me with the passion that drives youth to its follies. I ate too much at dinner. (*Points.*) My glass child. My maid Dorothea, the vixen, puts it out of my reach.

ROSE (*hands her the glass*). Your son killed her.

LADY ARE. My son? O I've slopped the glass! (*Chokes.*) Dear me. Thump my back child. (ROSE *pats her back.*) Thump I say! Lay on! O 'tis good! The seizure will take me. (*Wipes her eyes.*) Swear 'tis true! I must have my coach at dawn to tell the town.

ROSE. Thank you ma'am. I was afraid you wouldn't believe me.

LADY ARE. Believe ye? 'Tis the easiest thing to believe since the bishop of London's wife gave birth to a child with his chaplain's nose. I can't pay your husband – but you shall have the guinea.

ROSE. Lord Are says you've got us a pardon.

LADY ARE. Pox on the rogue! I haven't seen him since the day his father died. He snatched the pillow from under his head, bounded downstairs (one at a time, he had heels on), threw it at me, yowlped Hurrah! and hounded me from the house. (*Drinks.*) Come, see. (*Takes a huge pile of papers from her bosom.*) Shares, letters, promissory notes. All his. (*Wheezes as she fondles the papers.*) Look, forty thousand pounds. (*Paper.*) A half share in Jamaica. (*Paper.*) That would pay his pox pills. (*Paper.*) A castle in Scotland. (*Kisses papers and puts them back in her dress.*) Home to my heart, darlings. (*Paper.*) A letter from the Prime Minister to the Primate of England. You could blackmail him with this till he had to raise the income tax to pay you – and still have the Primate's reply. (*Paper.*) And this – a charge on his old foe Lester. (*Laughs and stuffs papers away.*) Back to the bosom that gave him suck (one Wednesday when the wet nurse was late) but now makes amends by making him starve. (*Smoothes her dress.*) They go with me to the grave and angels do not lie on softer down.

ROSE. He says the pardon's already –

LADY ARE. Pardon, pardon – cease with your pardons! My glass. There are no pardons.

ROSE. But you can get one?

LADY ARE. 'Tis true my figure sets a fashion few could follow – but the prince always liked a lady of carriage. He'd bed me still but his flesh is wore out with paint. His servants daub it on when they're drunk and he's too blind to wipe it off. Last week his whiskers were plastered to his cheeks with cold cream. They carry him round the palace in a sedan chair. He looks out of the window like a monkey sticking out of its jungle. A pardon? – nothing would be easier. 'Twould be as if the monkey reached up, plucked a banana from a tree and threw it into my lap. But I shall not ask.

ROSE. But Lady Are my husband's innocent!

LADY ARE. True, but he hath put out that he is not. Let him hang for a boaster. Child, who would be safe? Charles my footman would strangle me at table for the sake of a titbit on my plate, Dorothea would crack me over the head with my bottle and drink it, and Trevor my valet would kick me downstairs. Pardon? Ye might as well ask me to lead a riot or open a revolution.

ROSE. My husband is innocent.

LADY ARE. Then let him go to heaven. If he stays in this world he will go to hell with the rest of the footmen. If Society protest every time the law is an ass no one will respect it. I've watched lambs as innocent as driven snow go to the gallows and my head was not one hair the whiter. Console yourself. My son will hang. Stab Lester at cards or step on his toe at a hop. They'll brawl and one will be stabbed and the other hanged.

ROSE. My husband is good and kind and –

LADY ARE. I like him more and more.

ROSE (*kneels*). I beg you.

LADY ARE. Get up child. A thing is not made more impressive by being said by a dwarf. The ground is what we have risen from. Up! Ye made an old lady merry with a farce and now ye mar it with a wailing play!

ROSE. You bitch! I hope you fall downstairs! Choke! Die of gin! Have your head cracked with a bottle! And get pox from yer monkey!

    ROSE *goes*.

LADY ARE. The wretch hath a tongue on her like Dorothea, but she would have stayed for the guinea. I forgot to get the details! (*Calls*.) Dorothea! – Coupling with the kitchen boy again? Trevor! – The wretch is drunk! Hush, I'll invent the details. The papers said 'twas at table. She empties his plate on his head, peas and potatoes stream down his face and French coat and he runs her through and slips on a pudding and turns cartwheels while she – O! Ho! Ha! (*Laughs and wheezes.*) her – her – O! I shall be in bed for a week! Peace think of something else! – her last breath blows bubbles in the soup! (*She laughs.*) O! Hoo! Ha! (*Stops.*) The cold wind round my heart ... The turbot. The doctor forbade it. (*Wipes her mouth.*) The cream sauce ... I am an old woman with an empty glass and there is nothing to think of that does not wring me with regret for the past, convulse me at the follies of the present, or make me tremble before what is to come. I have not always lived after the precepts. 'Twould do no harm to prepare for heaven. Pah! a morbid thought. 'Twould drive my son to distraction – that is heaven, and I shall be the *deus ex machina* in it. As in the old romances, he shall be reprieved at the tree. I might send a copy direct to that scoundrel my son and give him the misery of reading it.

The Fair Tree of Liberty (ROSE *and* FRANK)

On the fair tree of liberty
The fruit weighs the branches to the ground
And look! the fruit are eyes
At the stealthy tread they open to see
The robber who comes to rob the tree
He turns around and runs
The eyes are brighter than a hundred suns

On the fair tree of liberty
The fruit weighs the branches to the ground
And look! the fruit are eyes
At the marching tread they open to see
The axeman who comes to fell the tree
He turns around and runs
The eyes are brighter than a hundred suns

On the fair tree of liberty
The fruit weighs the branches to the ground
And look! the fruit are eyes
At the heavy tread they open to see
The headsman who comes to burn the tree
He turns around and runs
The eyes are brighter than a thousand suns

Deep in the trunk bees murmur like thunder
High in the crown birds call
Telling the names of the passers-by
The eyes watch them as they come
And sometimes the branches rise and strike them down like
    bolts of thunder

And so the fair tree grows
As tall as the pine and strong as the oak
Wreathed with the climbing honeysuckle
The wild rose and the hanging vine
As our forefathers spoke

Scene Ten

Hilgay.
The Hall.
Breakfast Room.
ARE. *For the first time he is seen in a shirt and breeches and without a wig.*

ARE. Let a man have a fine day for his hanging. 'Tis morose to say otherwise. An empty house, all gone for the best places. How pleasantly the sun shines in at my windows to bless me. This morning I asked after a noise. 'Twas a lark.

I would have sung too but I lacked an orchestra. Flowers nodded, lambs bleated. Peter Sigh the poet would have –

MOTHER *comes in.*

MOTHER. Gentleman.
ARE. Not so downcast Hedges. I tried. The law is a heavy stone for one man to move.
MOTHER. Say it's urgent.
ARE. Tell him no.
MOTHER. Hev a letter.
ARE. O let him deliver. 'Tis a small cloud, 'twill pass.

MOTHER *goes.*

Now to the business of the day: clothes. (*Sighs.*) A suit so sober it seems I shop at a monastery. I tell the truth: I shall be glad when the day is past, when those who are to suffer have suffered and the rest may enjoy themselves as the world desires, without the mournful countenance a christian must spoil his hat with on these occasions.

MOTHER *comes in with the* MESSENGER. *She goes.*

MESSENGER. My lord, your mother's compliments.
ARE. Damme the she-goat repents! The hag's at death's door!
MESSENGER. My lord, my commission is urgent.

The MESSENGER *hands* ARE *a document.* ARE *reads it.*

ARE. Handsome. So Bob has his good news at last. To think he lieth in his pains and I hold in my hand his absolute and perfect liberty. 'Tis feathers to a bird. How the affairs of men stand on their heads!
MESSENGER. I must go to the prison.
ARE. Prison?
MESSENGER. That is a copy. I am commissioned to hand the original to the governor.

ARE. So you are – or it would go badly with Bob. Lookee
there is a great crowd about the roads. I'll take thee in my
coach.

MESSENGER. 'Tis kind my lord, but I am commissioned to –

ARE. Commission the pox! Would ye deny me my pleasure?

MESSENGER. Yes sir. I am commissioned to take –

ARE. But now I think on't I cannot take ye. I have my Lady
Oxy to sit beside me and her mother the Duchess of Blare
to sit opposite and the Duchess will have Lucille her maid.
Now Lucille is an absolute termagant, an hysteric who
rules the Duchess with a rod of iron and will have no man
near her. The Duchess was on the point of saying I must
run behind and hang onto the strap. The maid compro-
mised only because 'twas a hanging. A wedding or thanks-
giving and I should have wore out my shoe-leather pound-
ing the rear. So ye see sir ye cannot come in my coach even
if there was room. (*He has poured two cups of coffee. He
hands one to the* MESSENGER *and drinks the other*.) No sir
do not ask: ye may *not* sit on the roof. That's booked by
Lady Oxy's boys and their chums – for the boys will go to
the hangings. We shall have such a hallooing and hurrah-
ing as we fly through the lanes, such a stamping of feet on
the roof, such a throwing of the coachman's hat into the
duckponds ('tis only a matter of lettin' 'em grow up before
we go to *their* hangin') (MESSENGER *laughs*) – that
Lucille will have hysterics, sniff two bottles of smelling
salts dry and must lie down, miss the hangings and have
the Duchess fan her (the poor lady is tyrannised, 'tis a
scandal – and blackmail is rumoured) so that we hear
nothing but the maid's complaints all the way back, when
the rest of the company (in the natural circle of friendship)
wish to discuss the drop and each give his version of the last
confession, in one of which he will protest he is as innocent
as the unborn lamb and in another claim to have been a

highwayman from the age of ten. No sir I will not take ye in
the coach for the journey there will be so like the journey to
hell ye'd change places with Bob sooner than enter it for
the journey back.

MESSENGER (*putting the cup on the table*). No matter sir. My
commission demands that I –

ARE. Yet my conscience fears ye will not get through the
mob.

MESSENGER. As to that sir, I'll shout 'Clear in the King's
name'!

ARE. Never do that! Nay if ye shout that I cannot let ye
through the door.

MESSENGER. Is the king not honoured here sir?

ARE. They will suspect ye bring a pardon and pull ye from
your horse. 'Twould spoil their day. They have travelled
the country since dawn, bought their pennorth of pies and
tuppence of beer and practised their song sheets. When a
man's hanged the rest of the day's theirs, for riot or sober
reflection. When he is not, they work.

MESSENGER. I'm grateful for the warning sir. I'll ride hard
with my mouth shut. Now my commission must –

ARE. Wait! (*Aside.*) Must I kill another before breakfast in
this room? I shall run out of Bobs.

MESSENGER. Good day sir –

ARE. I have it! I have it! It would go hard with thee to fail in
thy commission – I would not see thee and thine suffer it. I
cannot take you in my coach – but I may take the pardon.

MESSENGER. But sir my commission says –

ARE. Sir you surprise me! Thou hast dawdled long enough.
More delay and I must complain to thy officer. Here are
thirty guineas in gold. The bringer of good news is
rewarded.

MESSENGER. Thirty guineas!

ARE. 'Tis naught. Fly to the tavern and drink my health. 'Tis a commission. God bless thee. I must dress and jump about.

MESSENGER. I thank your lordship.

The MESSENGER *gives* ARE *the pardon and goes.*

ARE. Now sure I am looked on by a guardian angel – though from whence I know not! I hold in my hand his pardon. I shall not deliver it. What, no lightning stroke? No thunder? The sun does not stop in its course! Lookee Are: thou art a strange soul. I begin to like thee, and I might worship thee. Ye have talents, nay powers I knew not of! Why d'ye live in poverty and marry an ash-raker's daughter? Ye neglect the proper care of thyself. Why have ye not twenty houses? An army? A hundred women? Ye fear Lord this and fawn on Lady that, ye hack your way down the street with your cane – when ye might be carried along it on the backs of the mob! All shall change. There shall be a new world. (*Calls.*) Hedges! Lay out my blue coat and yellow hat. Nay, my pink with the purple plumes. Let us not add to Bob's woes: he shall see a good hat at his hanging. Faith 'tis so spectacular 'twill take his mind off the rope. I shall doff it to the hangman – but Bob may take it as a courtesy to himself. Let the Great Boob hang to prove the world's in its senses. Besides, 'tis heartless to deny a mob. *Noblesse oblige*: Hang him.

Yet I grow fond! Think, I cannot ride up with the pardon! I must forgo the hanging! I take not the coach. I say I go horse-back to go faster. On the way I fall. Racing and hollooing with the joy of glad tidings, over I go tippity-top – knocked out. When I get to my feet the jade hath run. (I shall whip her off. 'Tis a faithful beast and will cling – but I'll break my whip on her, and if that don't serve throw stones.) Then I have my limp. (*Practises.*) Nay severer. (*Practises as he talks.*) I hobble (I have cut a stick from the hedge) to a nearby farm. Deserted. All at the hanging. We have not seen such desolation since the black death. On I crawl. Till time hath run out and poor Bob the Boob is led under the tree. He looks up at heaven – in the direction of the parson's finger – to the welcoming face of god: and all he sees is the black beam above him. I sit in the hedge and weep. Yea, I uncover my head and kneel in the nettles and pray: for the rope to break.

O thou great blazing sun! Great fire of ever-lasting day! My life! My ministering star! Blaze! Blaze! Blaze! Blaze! Hail great sun! Light of the world that I shall stride in! . . . O my friends –

MOTHER *comes in.*

MOTHER. Blue an' pink's laid out.
ARE. Hedges. Rest in thy chamber.
MOTHER. Keep busy. Cry for him last night, cry later.
ARE. Mothers know best. Lookee, light a fire against my return. The day might yet be cold. Warm thy old hands at the blaze. Here is a paper to start it. (*He gives her the pardons.*)

ARE *goes.*

MOTHER. Kind on him. Save me fetch the kindlin'. Official. Pretty crown on top. Cut them out for Christmas decoration. (*Shakes her head.*) Best do what yoo're towd. Bob was learnin' to read. (*Tears the papers.*) Ont start that doo yoo ont git the work out the way.

MOTHER *starts the fire.*

ARE (*off*). Hedges!
MOTHER (*sighing to herself as she stoops – she has become much older*). Now what?

ARE *comes in shouting.*

ARE. 'Tis too much! Hedges will ye make me a fool! Dress me in motley? Set me up as a clown?

MOTHER (*Calm, flat*). Sir whatever is the –

ARE. Damned impertinence! Can a man trust nothing! I kept your man when I might have celebrated my title by sacking him! Are you as blind as he?

MOTHER (*calm, flat*). Now sir I'm sure there's no call to –

ARE. No, ye did it on purpose! Petty revenge! (*Holds out his blue coat.*) Where is the button! D'ye see it? No! 'Tis off! (*Throws his blue coat on the floor.*) Here, here (*Thumps his chest.*) where every fool can see it! You ancient hag must I sew it myself? I give ye the roof over your head, the ground under your feet, the food on your plate – for a gaping hole with two black spots and a white thread like the lower-anatomy of a mouse! An idiot's badge!

MOTHER. Give it here, I'll see to –

ARE. Now? When it lies in the filth? (*The floor must be filthy since I have not swept it today.*) I must dress like a tramp! O she will sew the button now the coat can't be worn! (*Kicks the coat.*) Madam sew it on and throw the coat in the kennels for my bitch to whelp on. Let her at least have the respect of a full set of buttons. (*Suddenly becomes his old self again.*) Now I must wear my green. So I cannot wear my pink. Twould look like a maypole. I must wear my yellow – which I wore twice at the races. (*Aside.*) 'Tis true I can't go to the hanging. But now the whole county will say 'twas because I could not afford a new hat!

ARE *goes.* MOTHER *mutters to herself as she goes back to the fire.*

MOTHER. Can't sew it on. Ont give me the button.

Suddenly (BOB)

It came suddenly like a bomb
They didn't die with the gestures of dying
They didn't cover their heads in fear
They didn't lift their hands in supplication
They died with the gestures of living

It came suddenly like a bomb
Mouths were open but the words were not spoken
The salt was lifted but wasn't shaken
They died with the gestures of living
Fingers beckoned and hands stretched out to feel
Heads leaned forward in concentration
On words they would never hear

So sudden was the disaster
So swift the moment of fate
It fell at the time of the midday meal
When the fork was halfway between
The mouth and the plate.

Scene Eleven

Peterborough.
Holme Cottage. A beer barrel.
MRS WILSON *and* BOB.
BOB *is in shirt sleeves and without fetters. He drinks at the table.*

BOB. When woman? (MRS WILSON *fills his glass. He grabs her arm.*) She's a sly one.
WILSON. Behave or I'll tell Mr Wilson.
BOB (*lets her arm go*). His nibs is quiet. He'll hev to come down for my pardon.

WILSON. Let him sleep. I pulled his door to so he shan't be disturbed.

BOB (*shouts at the ceiling*). Who's in the land of nod? Shh!

WILSON. I'll confiscate your glass.

BOB. Phew. Had enough. Powerful stuff.

WILSON. On your feet. Put your jacket on. Sit there in your shirt sleeves.

BOB (*stands, staggers slightly, steadies himself with one hand on the table*). Oops.

WILSON (*buttons*). Fasten you in.

BOB. Us'll shake hands. Thankyoo sir. Hope yoo hev the same one day. (*Giggles.*) Think when they see how posh I am they most likely give me two pardons.

WILSON. I'll top you up.

BOB (*flat palm over the glass*). Nope. Ont drink 'n'more.

PARSON *and* ROSE *come in*.

Rose! My gal. How I hev miss you. (*Kiss.*) There – thass better now. All's turn out well. The terrible times are over. (*Whispers to* ROSE.) Mrs Wilson say it's come today. Sh! – Parson yoo let your faith wobble but yoo'll git a surprise. Mrs Wilson do the man the honours an' pour his drink. (*Wipes the glass clean on his sleeve.*) Drat spoil me coat. (*Hands the glass to* MRS WILSON.) The letters swim in my head like thass a shipwreck.

PARSON (*low*). Mrs Wilson a drink for his spirits is one thing. But to do this at such an hour is cruel. Wrong. A needless adding to his burdens.

WILSON. I don't need a sermon on how to run a gaol. The profit I make on this it's not worth buying in. (*Gives him the glass.*) No doubt you'll take your glass parson?

PARSON (*slight embarrassment*). Yes yes, thank you. His and my way go differently today.

MRS WILSON *keeps a tally of the beer that is drunk. She marks it on a slate with chalk.*

BOB. Rose is ought wrong? (*She has her back to him. He turns her. Her face is showered in tears. He steps back.*) That ... ont tears of joy ... (*Vaguely.*) Why'm I wearin' my best jacket? My pardon come today ...

PARSON (*hands him an open prayer book*). Read your prayers to me.

BOB. Ont want a lesson!

WILSON (*to* ROSE). Hand me his glass.

BOB. Ay! Less drink! Sorry parson. Why's this gloom fall all around? Rose, ont make my heart sick to see yoo cry. Rose I only lent his lordship my name.

The PARSON *has three prayer-books open at The Burial of the Dead. He reads and recites Psalm 39 continuously (interrupting himself only once) and the rest of the scene goes on round him. He finally stops reading when he says 'At last. Better. He comes to thee'. After that he prays silently. As the* PARSON *reads from his own book he offers* BOB *the second book open at the place.* BOB *snatches this and throws it on the ground.*

Ont pray at me! Ont be hanged!

The PARSON *picks up the book while he reads his own.*

Drunk! (*Empties his drink on the floor but does not throw the mug.*)

WILSON. O I see we're going to have one of those days. – He should have been told properly. It's not decent treating him like this. – Bobby sit down. Crying won't help.

BOB (*stares at* MRS WILSON). Woman what yoo done? ... Yoo towd me my pardon was ... (*Sudden idea.*) Ah!

BOB lurches out. MRS WILSON goes on her knees and mops up the beer.

WILSON. Mrs Hedges stand by him or go outside.
ROSE. He's innocent.
WILSON. They all are if you listen long enough.

Crash upstairs.

There goes the door. That'll cost someone. All this fuss! You come here and behave as if I had nothing better to do.

Crash upstairs.

WILSON (*shouting up*). You wicked boy! (*To the others.*) It's my husband's job. He'll expect his dinner when he gets home. I wish you'd stop cluttering up my kitchen.
BOB (*off*). Ah!
WILSON. There'll be the dickens to pay.
BOB (*off*). Bed made. Cold.

GAOLER *comes in with* FRANK.
FRANK *is drunk.*

GAOLER. Cart's outside ma'am. Jist git the horse in.
FRANK (*morose, almost inaudible*).
Old Samson had a daughter, her name was Isabelle
The lily of the valley and the primrose of the dell

When she went a-walking she choosed me for her guide
Down by the Arun river to watch the fishes glide
FRANK (*Sees* BOB *through the door*). Two of Bob. Have to hang twice.

BOB *comes in.*

BOB. So I'm to hang. Skinned alive. Rose what'll us do? (*Tries to think. Turns to* PARSON.) Howd his row or I crack his head! (PARSON *prays uninterruptedly.*)

GAOLER. Goo quiet or goo shackled, you hev the choice. (*Pours drinks and raises glass.*) Drink to both gents. Wish I could drink to better times. (*Drinks.*)

BOB. Curses! That a man dies so! Git Are here! That blackguard! Why doo he doo this? When was I angry at him? When did I raise my fist? Touch cap – work quiet – bow – ont that enough? Now he want my head!

FRANK.
The first three months were scarcely o'er,
The young gal lost her bloom
The red fell from her bonny cheeks
And her eyes began to swoon

PARSON (*to* BOB). O do not deny yourself the comfort of his word.

BOB. Yes Frank sing! Kiss me Rose! Yoo ont ashamed of me. How I doo love thee! Ont miss the world: miss thee. (*Jumps onto the table.*) Shall we hang? Then hang so high! (*Points up.* FRANK *tries to climb onto the table with him.*)

BOB *and* FRANK.
The next nine months was passed and gone
She brought forth to me a son
And I was quickly sent for
To see what could be done
FRANK (*continues alone*).
I said I should marry her
But o! that would not be
PARSON (*tapping* FRANK *on the back*). My friend open your heart –

FRANK. Git off me yer sinful old bugger! I'll open you!

FRANK *snatches the prayer-books and throws them away.*

The GAOLER *moves in. The* PARSON *motions him back.
He closes his eyes and goes on reciting the prayers aloud by
heart.* BOB *notices nothing of this but comes down from the
table.*

WILSON (*pouring beer*). Four. I keep count so no one's over-
charged. (*To* ROSE.) They're allowed one in the cart. I'd
offer, but now there's the door to pay . . . (*Pours drinks for
everyone.*)

Drum Song (BOB)

A drummer beat upon a drum
And no sound came
He hit the skin
He struck the skin
And no sound came
Wild in his frenzy
A madman sweating blood
He beat he struck he hammered blows
And no sound came
He thrashed and lashed
All through the night
And on into the light
Till his hands bled
Till his eyes bled
Till blood ran from his ears
Till the teeth shook in his head
Till the bones rattled in his body like dice
And still he made no sound
He struck with sticks of iron
With sticks of bone
With sticks of steel
He staggered
He began to reel
In pain

He hammered on
Again! Again!
He crawled upon the ground
He flailed the drum lashed to his side
And no sound came
From the beaten hide
He did not stop till he was dead
   And other men are silent
   When they labour them
   About the head

BOB. The pardon'll come on the square. I can't be so lied to. Rose I'm scared to die. (*Holds her.*)

PARSON. At last. Better. He comes to thee. (*Kneels and prays silently.*)

FRANK. God rot yer Bobby Hedges! I'll pay to go second an' see yer swing. There's justice in this! Yer dragged me to the gallows, yer rantin' hypocrite! Remember the mornin'? If I'd gone with the knife an' fork an' spoon I wouldn't have took the rest! Twelve knives. Ten spoons. Eighteen forks. I'd have been careful then. No drinkin' an' whorin'. Made me way to London like a sane man. Gone round a corner for ever. Safe. Home. The rope don't stretch that far. I hope yer hanging's a cruel one. Yer live to cry mercy on the rope an' don't get it!

   He falls down.

GAOLER (*calling to outside*). She playin' yoo up?

ROSE. Drink. (*Gets glass.*) Bobby.

   BOB *takes the glass and gulps it down.* MRS WILSON *refills* BOB's *glass and holds him as* ROSE *pours it into his mouth.*

PARSON. Mrs Wilson I'll lodge a complaint.

   GAOLER *picks* FRANK *up and lays him over the barrel.*

ROSE (*tilts* BOB's *head back and pours drink drown his throat*).
Drink. Drink. Drink.

PARSON. No! Let him feel the pain or god's anger is not
slaked!

WILSON (*to* BOB). Mr Wilson will help you. You were kind
to him. He won't hurt you. It doesn't take long.

GAOLER (*calling to the outside*). Ready?

BOB (*pushing the glass away*). No. Ont. Clear head. Speak. In
square. Innocent. Englishman. Are's murderer. Murder
me. English.

PARSON. Nay! Who can believe a man who speaks so
harshly? I forbid you to name his lordship. Have you no
gratitude?

BOB. Ay? Ay? Gratitude they want? . . . What can I say? . . .
Who'll hear all I can say?

GAOLER. Pay no heed parson. They say all sorts – (*To* BOB.)
and out there no one listen. They'll shortly give yoo cause
to wish yoo'd saved yoor breath.

VOICE (*off*). She's in.

BOB (*shakes his head to clear it. Then, aside to audience*). I ont
believe this.

> GAOLER *takes* BOB *and* FRANK *out.* FRANK *sings. The*
> PARSON *picks up the three prayer-books and puts on his*
> *last vestments as he follows the others out.*

WILSON. You can lie down upstairs. Bed's made. Clear this
mess away. Wish Mr Wilson didn't have to go out today.
When he's had a turn he's nervous. The young man's
waiting for something to go wrong. Then he'll step in.
Some of them would push you in the river to get your job.

> ROSE *has followed the others out.* MRS WILSON *checks the*
> *amount she has sold.*

Scene Twelve

London Bridge.
ROSE.

ROSE. I stand on London Bridge. Bodies float in the sky and sink towards the horizon. Crocodiles drift in the Thames. On the embankment the plane trees rattle their fingers. Men walk the streets with chains hanging from their mouths. Pillars of black smoke rise between the towers and the temples. The stars will come out like scabs on the sky. There is a gentle breeze.

What have I learned? If nothing, then *I* was hanged.

Man is What He Knows (ROSE)

Does the judge say
I send your arms to prison today
But your feet are free
To walk away?

Does the boss buy
The apple core from the market stall
And leave the skin?
He buys it all

Do the troops shoot
To kill your stomach but not your head?
They shoot to kill
You drop down dead

Once Satan roamed the earth to find
Souls that money could buy
Now he comes to steal your mind
He doesn't wait till you die

The houses burn on the edge of the town
'It's only the dawn – we can tell'
When it reaches your house you will fight
Like the men locked in their cell

Man is what he knows – or doesn't know
The empty men reap death and sow
Famine wherever they march
But they do not own the earth
Sooner believe I could strike it a blow
With my fist and miss!

Geese fly over the moon and do not know
   That for a moment they fill the world with
     beauty
      Flakes do not know where they drive in
       the storm
        But each flake falls to the earth
         below
          And in the morning shines in the
           world of snow
            Wind and rain cannot tell where
             they blow
              But we may know who we
               are and where we go

I say these things for me and Bob Hedges. I must have one
hand of iron and the other of steel. There is a gentle breeze
from the city. I cross the bridge and go into the streets.

End

Notes

1) This is the PARSON's prayer for Scene Eleven:
I said, I will take heed to my ways: that I offend not in my

tongue. I will keep my mouth as it were with a bridle: while the ungodly is in my sight. I held my tongue, and spake nothing! I kept silence, yea, even from good words; but it was pain and grief to me. My heart was hot within me, and while I was thus musing the fire kindled: and at last I spake with my tongue; Lord, let me know mine end, and the number of my days: that I may be certified how long I have to live. Behold, thou hast made my days as it were a span long: and mine age is even as nothing in respect of thee; and verily every man living is altogether vanity. For man walketh in a vain shadow, and disquieteth himself in vain: he heapeth up riches, and cannot tell who shall gather them. And now, Lord, what is my hope: truly my hope is even in thee. Deliver me from all mine offences: and make me not a rebuke unto the foolish. I became dumb, and opened not my mouth: for it was thy doing. Take thy plague away from me: I am even consumed by means of the heavy hand. When thou with rebukes dost chasten man for sin, thou makest his beauty to consume away, like as it were a moth fretting a garment: every man therefore is but vanity. Hear my prayer, O Lord, and with thine ears consider my calling: hold not thy peace at my tears. For I am a stranger with thee: and a sojourner, as all my fathers were. O spare me a little, that I may recover my strength: before I go hence, and be no more seen. Glory be to the Father, and to the Son: and to the Holy Ghost; as it was in the beginning, is now, and ever shall be: world without end. Amen.

2) The music for FRANK's song in Scene Eleven is 'Bogie's Bonnie Belle'.

The Cat

A story for music

CAST

Cats:

LORD PUFF
ARNOLD, *his nephew*
JONES, *the money lender*
TOM
PETER, *Tom's friend*
MINETTE
BABETTE, *Minette's sister*
LOVERS

The following respectable citizens and members of the RSPR:

MR KEEN
MR FAWN
MR PLUNKETT
MISS CRISP
MRS GOMFIT
LADY TOODLE

Mouse:

LOUISE

Dogs:

JUDGE
COUNSEL FOR THE PROSECUTION
COUNSEL FOR THE DEFENCE

Birds:

JURY
PARSON

Fox:

LUCIAN

From the sky:

MOON
STARS

London about 1900

Part One

Scene One

Mrs Halifax's drawing-room

LORD PUFF, ARNOLD, LOUISE, MR KEEN, MR FAWN, MR PLUNKETT, MISS CRISP, MRS GOMFIT, LADY TOODLE.

PUFF. My youth passed and I did not think of marriage. I loved the poor and needy. Now Mrs Halifax has spoken: a cat of my breeding must not pass without issue. Mrs Halifax is our mistress: her word is law. Today the young lady she has chosen for my spouse comes from the country. Dear friends I have asked you here to meet her and give your approval.

KEEN. A risky step.

FAWN. We may sometimes be pardoned for falling into error.

MISS CRISP. Cats of older years should show discretion.

PLUNKETT.
MRS GOMFIT. } If Mrs Halifax has spoken it must be done.

ARNOLD.
Eve was a thief and since her time
The female sex has lived on crime
Adam was tempted – when he fell
His paradise turned into hell
The fruit of Eve became his curse
He lost his heart and soul and purse
She stole the apple from the tree
Then stole her husband's property

No woman's born without a flaw
She is a bitch or shrew or whore

She looks as lovely as a saint –
Sainthood from a pot of paint
A youth has time to change his wife
An old bridegroom is stuck for life

PLUNKETT. Let us pray for guidance for our dear friend
Puff.

ALL.

The ways of god are hid from man
We cannot tell the master's plan
The pen is weaker than the sword
And truth is just a little word
But our's is not to question god
Humbly we kneel before the rod

The skylarks singing in the sky
Are broken by the storms and die
The daisies blooming in the grass
Are trodden by the beasts that pass
And god ordains that man must wed
And find his first grave in the bed

    A knock at the door.

KEEN. A knock!
FAWN. A timid one.
MISS CRISP. That sounds promising.
PUFF (*combing his hair*). O dear.
MRS GOMFIT. Lord Puff such worldliness!
PUFF. It is my duty – however troublesome to myself – to
make myself presentable to the young lady.
PLUNKETT. Answer the door.
PUFF. Perhaps she's gone. We cannot run after her in
the street. If god ordains we are not to meet – so be
it. O!

    ARNOLD *opens the door.* BABETTE *comes in.*

BABETTE. Good day. I am looking for Lord Puff.

MISS CRISP. A rather ordinary young woman.

FAWN. Quite plain by London standards.

MRS GOMFIT. A certain country freshness.

PLUNKETT. That won't put too much temptation in Puff's way.

MRS GOMFIT. Step forward child.

FAWN. How respectfully she bows.

LADY TOODLE. I think we may approve.

PUFF. Good day Miss Minette. I trust your journey was not too tiring.

BABETTE. I am Babette. Minette is my sister. She wanted me to see you first.

CRISP. Why?

BABETTE. To be sure you were respectable.

THE REST. Respectable? Good heavens!

PLUNKETT. We're up for approval!

MISS CRISP. There are no persons more responsible than we.

BABETTE. I will fetch Minette. She is very shy.

ARNOLD (*aside, while they wait for Minette*):
For years I pandered to this fool
I acted as his humble tool
I laughed at every stupid joke
And groaned beneath this heavy yoke
For I am very very broke

But when he died I'd be in heaven
(I hope he goes to hell)
I cannot pay my gambling debts
There's nothing left to sell
I am in an extremity
I'd even turn to pray
If god would promise me

That when he died I'd be
My uncle's heir

> MINETTE *comes in. She is very pretty.*

ALL *except* MINETTE
and BABETTE. O.

BABETTE. Minette – Lord Puff.

PUFF. Good day Miss Minette. I trust your journey was not too tiring?

MINETTE. How do you do. I have never seen so big a city or so many people sir. To one of my innocence it is a little alarming.

ARNOLD (*aside*): My uncle is lost. And so is my money.

MINETTE. I was not afraid. Before I left our village the parson told me this.

The world is wide and there are many corners
In which the prince of darkness sets his snares
And waits to trap poor innocent young maidens
Who set out on life's journey unawares

When danger threatens child look up to heaven
And call for help – god's waiting in the skies
He feeds the poor and shelters little orphans
And answers every innocent who cries

LADY TOODLE. Minette we are godly people.

PLUNKETT. All of us are members of the Royal Society for the Protection of Rats.

BABETTE. Rats?

KEEN. It is the cat's duty to protect rats.

FAWN. Too long they have suffered at our hands.

BABETTE. What do you eat?

MRS GOMFIT. Food descends from heaven on a plate.

BABETTE. Not in our house. In the country we hunt.

LADY TOODLE. Even in England there are corners still not civilised.

MISS CRISP. It is our mission to convert them.

MRS GOMFIT. Louise!

LOUISE *comes forward*.

LOUISE. I am an orphan mouse. One day a ginger Tom ate mama and papa and my twelve brothers and sixteen sisters and my ten aunts and seven uncles and grandmama and grandpapa and great grandmama and great grandpapa and all my –

MISS CRISP (*sweetly*): This will take all day.

KEEN. Get on my dear.

FAWN. It was not an English cat.

KEEN. A stow-away on a continental vessel.

LADY TOODLE. Carrying wine.

LOUISE. I was rescued by the RSPR. I said farewell to the corpses of my little family. I was sent to school and taught to miaow.

SONG

Out from its hole a little mouse
Crept into this cruel world
And on it like a thunderbolt
A great big tom cat hurled

Its teeth were knives! Its claws were hooks!
It was about to kill
When from on high a voice spake forth
'O cruel cat be still

Its little heart beats just like yours
It shares the selfsame woe
It loves its parent and its child
O do not hurt it so!'

Remorse then struck the cruel cat
He said 'Pray have no fears'
Instead of gobbling up the mouse
It licked away its tears

LOUISE *holds out an RSPR collecting box.*

Miaow!

BABETTE. Rubbish! The poor cats would starve!

ARNOLD (*aside*): I begin to hope. Minette, no doubt you agree with your sister?

MINETTE. No sir. The parson said I must always agree with my husband. His wife said he was right.

BABETTE.

Fox eats hen and cat eats rat
And the world is round not flat
We live by this inhuman law
And fight with bloody tooth and claw
Because we're hungry, cold and poor

ARNOLD. Uncle you must not marry into this evil family.

PUFF.

Arnold where is your charity?
The child is in danger
I must marry her and teach her Christian ways
She's as entitled to our love
As is the snow white dove

Hush! no more agitation
It has been a tiring day
I am to be married
This is a time for meditation
Searching for salvation
Reflecting on predestination
Excuse me while I pray

PUFF *falls asleep.*

BABETTE. Minette! We do not belong here! These people will do us harm! Let us go!

ENSEMBLE

BABETTE.
My sister this is not a place
Where you can be contented
If mother knew the things they say
She would not have consented
For you to leave us in this way
And wed a cat that won't eat mice
But lives on nuts and fruit and rice

MINETTE.
O parson when I was at home
Why did you preach to me
That when I called for help
A hand would reach to me
And lift me from despair?
For now I call for help
I cannot see
A helping hand – not anywhere

KEEN, FAWN, PLUNKETT, MISS CRISP, MRS GOMFIT, LADY TOODLE, LOUISE (*individually and together*).
The devil passes through the world
He looks upon the misery he makes
On all who weep and groan in this dark place
But he is never seen
He hides behind the smile
That never leaves his face

ARNOLD.
Do not trust her
She will do evil
She's sent here by the devil

> PUFF *snores*.

> MINETTE *goes in confusion, leaving the others as they sing*.

Scene Two

The roof of Mrs Halifax's house

Night. Stars and moon. MINETTE *comes on. From the distance lovers are heard serenading.*

LOVERS.
O love you sigh as softly as the waves
On pools at night
Where branches touch the water
In a deep delight
And on them silver droplets lie
Like opals on a negress' thigh

A shadow passes on the shore
Over the water to the boat
Which seems upon a silver sea to float
And its white sail is full of dreams

As you lie at my side again
The naked moon high in the night
Throws down her light and the dark pool
Is struck by silver rain

TOM *and* PETER *come on.*

TOM *and* PETER.
When work is done and you are young
There's a dance to be danced
A song to be sung
A breast to hold
A sigh to sigh
A whore to be paid
And a tale to be told
Of the way of a man with a maid

For in so short a time
Callow youth is sallow age
The young die in their prime
Youth fades before it's old
So learn to live in bed
Before you lie in it dead

TOM. Peter look! (*To* MINETTE.) What's your name?

MINETTE. Gentlemen this roof is the property of Mrs
Halifax. You are trespassing.

PETER. Do you live here miss?

MINETTE. It is the residence of my fiance Lord Puff.

PETER (*to* TOM): Too young! It would take too long!

    TOM *and* PETER *go.*

MINETTE. Those voices were so beautiful that I am sure I
ought not to have listened. The parson told me not to listen
to anything I didn't understand. Then I could not be led
astray. How silly to run away from my husband on the day
we meet. I ought to go down.

    TOM *comes back as she sings.*

O moon you pass so calmly in the sky
What acts of folly you have seen!
The madman's cry, the killer's rage
The clown laugh on his little stage
And men with power for a day destroy an age
And send their sons to die
Yet are not grey with weariness
Or red with shame
But of one whiteness constantly the same
O tell me why?

TOM. I came to apologise.

MINETTE. Thankyou. (*Going.*) Please excuse me.

TOM. How beautiful!

MINETTE (*aside*): Thank heavens the parson warned me against such men. (*To* TOM:) Sir I do not wish to subscribe to a magazine or purchase an encyclopaedia or any household article, nor do I need to be converted or intend to join a political party.

TOM. My name is Tom. What is your name?

MINETTE. I will tell you if you promise to go.

TOM. I promise!

MINETTE. Minette.

TOM. Ah! Now I cannot go!

MINETTE. Why not?

TOM.

Last night I dreamed I was in bed
A fever raging in my head
The doctor shook my hand and went
The parson sighed and said repent
My heart was faint
My mouth was dry
My face was wet
With ice-cold sweat
I was about to die
And then an angel fell
Out of the sky
And with a kiss she made me well
I asked her name
She said Minette

Thank heaven I have met you!

MINETTE. Why? You are not ill.

TOM. I am on fire! Touch me!

MINETTE. The parson said I must not touch anyone. Not even myself if at all possible.

TOM. Have pity!

MINETTE. If he behaved like this in the country we would

say he was ill. But in London all behave so strangely. It is
difficult to see his face. I believe he is handsome and so I
must not trust him.

DUET

TOM.
Why does beauty bring desire?
This strange power to destroy
To drag us through the mire
Or give the greatest joy!
We sell the poor man's blood
To pay a whore in gold
And when for beauty's sake one day
All that we had is sold
Still for one night or less
We throw our life away
MINETTE.
A man will waste his life and cross the world
And sift the grains of sand
Upon each windy strand
And pour them from his trembling hand
To find one little shell
In which he thinks he hears
The music of the spheres
Which is the song of hell
TOM (*throws himself at* MINETTE's *feet*). Minette I love you!

ARNOLD *creeps onto the roof.*

MINETTE. Tom that makes me so happy.
ARNOLD (*aside*): Excellent! A scandal is about to occur.
MINETTE. Who knows more than I how inappropriate my
marriage to Lord Puff would be?
TOM. I do.
ARNOLD (*aside*): Good. They are going to be really wicked.

MINETTE. But you have saved me.

TOM (*sees* ARNOLD). Scoundrel! Clear off!

ARNOLD (*aside*): Its unchristian to quarrel. Anyway I've seen enough.

TOM *chases* ARNOLD *out*.

TOM (*shouting after him*): I'll break your neck!

MINETTE. Tom you are the victim of uncontrollable passions. All the better! My conquest is the greater! Tom kneel!

TOM *kneels*.

MINETTE. As I was saying: Lord Puff is a man of education and income with a large town house and the run of an estate in Scotland. I am nothing and I bring nothing. Now all is changed! On the very day I meet my husband I bring him my first convert!

TOM. First convert?

MINETTE. Yes – there will be many more. I hope you are not jealous? You are to join the RSPR. How happy I shall make Lord Puff!

TOM. This is another dream!

MINETTE. Tom! You must struggle with your animal nature. I shall always be on hand to help you. From this day on you will never ill-treat a rat.

TOM. No! Not if they suffer as I do!

TOM *runs away in despair*.

MINETTE (*calls*): Tom ... Tom ...

ENSEMBLE

MOON *and* STARS.
The moon walks naked through the night
Men gaze upon her beauty

Half blinded by the silver light
And see! the silver rain
Falls in the lake
And on the darkling water
Casts its silver stain

MINETTE.
Tom ... My voice echoes over the roofs of the city ...

MOON *and* STARS.
The oarsman stirs in sleep and now
The moon is dancing on the lake
The boat begins to rock and silver light
Shimmers from helm to prow

MINETTE.
Tom ... He does not answer ...

MOON *and* STARS.
On the dark lake a swan
Shot by a silver arrow lies
And sings as if she lay
In her young lover's arms
And singing dies

MINETTE.
Why am I moved when I think of his face? ...
Look ... a cloud is covering the moon ...

MOON *and* STARS.
My lover reaches from the bed
To draw the veil and then turns back to me
For what we do men must not see
Or staring at the rapture in the sky
They shudder at the coldness of their earth
And die

MINETTE.
... Tom ...

> MINETTE *goes.*

Scene Three

Mrs Halifax's private chapel

ARNOLD *and* MR JONES

ARNOLD (*aside*): Today my uncle marries and I shall lose my fortune. Mr Jones is my money-lender. He comes to threaten me.

PUFF *enters*.

ARNOLD. Uncle may I introduce my friend Jones? He is a doctor.

JONES (*bows*). Lord Puff I have the honour to make your – (*Stops.*) O.

PUFF. What is the matter?

JONES. Is your complexion always that colour?

PUFF. Certainly.

ARNOLD (*aside*): He has put on more powder for the ceremony.

JONES. And your eyes?

PUFF. What is wrong with my eyes?

JONES. O nothing sir. Pray stick out your tongue.

PUFF. I will not sir!

JONES (*turning away*). I merely thought that as a doctor . . .

PUFF (*tongue*). Whhsama'mawimython?

JONES. Put it away. (*Pats his brow with a handkerchief.*) I feel quite faint. (*Takes* PUFF's *pulse.*) Purely in the interests of scientific research sir. A full record of your case should be preserved. O dear o dear! Do not be alarmed! (*To* ARNOLD:) We must not agitate him. (*To* PUFF:) Don't get upset sir!

PUFF. Upset! Damnation sir I'm not upset!

JONES (*to* ARNOLD): If he lives a quiet life – early to bed – blinds drawn by day – then we may hope.

ARNOLD. Dr Jones this afternoon my uncle is to be married.

JONES (*folds hands*). Then the service will soon be followed by another of a different sort.

PUFF. But I feel perfectly well!

JONES. Classic symptoms of the disease of hyposymtochondriamania: a feeling of perfect health.

ARNOLD. Ah the scourge! – hyposymtochondriamania! Uncle be comforted: it doesn't run in families! I shall perpetuate our line!

PUFF. It's my duty to marry! I am to become president of the RSPR!

JONES. Reckless youth dies for a ribbon but a man of mellow age must not sacrifice himself even for a presidency.

ARNOLD. Uncle I forbid it!

The PARSON *and* MR PLUNKETT *enter.* TOM *follows. He is disguised as a curate.* PUFF *walks up and down in perplexity.*

HYMN

PARSON *and* PLUNKETT *and* TOM.
In Eden was created Eve
But for her sin the Lord decreed
That man henceforth should always breed
In darkness and not dwell
In Eden's bliss but hell

And it is well! Man plays his part!
He takes a wife
And clasps her to his heart
As if he held a knife

PUFF. Arnold I shall do my duty! You will be best man!

The priest and TOM *pray.* PLUNKETT *prepares the altar.*

ARNOLD (*aside to* JONES): Jones are you a true friend?

JONES. Much more: I am a creditor. I'll stick by you for the sake of my sixty thousand pounds. (*Goes to* PUFF.) Let me render your Lordship a service. (*Taps walking stick.*) Here is a pharmaceutical distillation of essential essences. This will get your lordship through the ceremony and the honeymoon . . .

> JONES *unscrews a glass from the top of the stick, removes a stopper from the stick and pours the cordial into the glass.*

JONES (*sniffs glass*). O virtuous potion! (*Wafts scent under his nose.*) Ah youth!

ARNOLD (*aside to* JONES): Will it finish him off?

JONES (*aside to* ARNOLD): Of course. He stands there piling up interest on your loan: and so he drains your life as surely as if he sucked blood from your throat.

ARNOLD (*aside*): Then it's only self-defence. (*Hands glass to* PUFF.) Uncle.

PUFF (*hesitates*). But . . .

JONES. The vital effluences will escape into the air. There is no more. The genius who made it died of an overdose at ninety-seven.

PUFF (*about to drink*). Well the atmosphere is a trifle heavy . . .

PLUNKETT. Wait!

PARSON. A walking-stick flask!

PLUNKETT. Allow me to inspect that concoction.

JONES. Purely medicinal!

PUFF (*hands glass to* PLUNKETT). Sir.

PLUNKETT (*sniffs*). Brandy!

ALL *except* JONES. Brandy!

JONES. A little brandy to disguise the taste. The other ingredients are very wholesome.

PARSON. Throw that devil's brew away!

> PLUNKETT *throws the potion from the window.*

JONES (*aside to* ARNOLD): Damn you and your uncle! I'll put the bailiffs in!

ARNOLD (*aside*): I am not yet defeated!

> *Enter* MINETTE *as a bride. She is attended by* BABETTE, MISS CRISP, MRS GOMFIT *and* LADY TOODLE.

HYMN

BRIDE'S ATTENDANTS.
The bride comes to the altar dressed in white
With flowers in her hair
She trembles in despair
Before the coming night

And it is well! She plays her part!
God's law must be obeyed
He laid his curse on man
And man must lie on maid

DOUBLE RECITATIVE

PARSON. I require and charge you both, as ye will answer at the dreadful day of judgement when the secrets of all hearts shall be disclosed, that if either of you know any impediment why ye may not be lawfully joined together in matrimony, ye do now confess it etc etc etc.

TOM. Ah to stand so near my angel that I could touch her! If she marries this fool I shall cut my throat and throw my carcass at her feet. But during the ceremony I hope to find a moment to pursuade her to elope.

ARNOLD. I object!

PARSON. You can't!

ARNOLD. Why not?

PARSON. You're best man!

ARNOLD (*to* MINETTE): Madam answer my questions!

PUFF. Arnold be silent!

BABETTE. Sir will you defame my sister's honour? (*To* MINETTE): I told you we should not stay in this city!

MINETTE. Arnold speak!

ARNOLD. Were you on the roof at night with a young man?

OTHERS. Young man!

MINETTE. Yes.

ARNOLD. In a bacchanalia?

OTHERS. A bacchanalia!

JONES (*aside*): The boy shows promise.

MINETTE. Yes.

ARNOLD. Did you speak of your marriage to uncle with despair?

OTHERS. Despair!

JONES (*aside*): Things are improving.

MINETTE. Yes.

ARNOLD. And did your gigolo –

OTHERS. Gigolo!

JONES (*aside*): We might be saved!

ARNOLD. – declare himself your slave? Wretched woman it would have been better if you had eloped!

OTHERS. Eloped!

JONES (*aside*): Now he's done it!

MINETTE. Yes –

OTHERS. O!

MINETTE. – I met Tom on the roof –

OTHERS. Wretched woman!

MINETTE. True he addressed me in a reckless manner.

OTHERS. Reckless!

JONES (*aside*): Nothing can save her.

MINETTE. To which I gave a friendly response.

OTHERS. She has no shame!

PUFF. Thank god this has been found out!

JONES (*aside*): I hear the clink of coins and the rustle of banknotes.

MINETTE. And why? To change Tom's heart and enrol him in the RSPR. Such was to be the wedding present I brought to my husband.

Ah cruel world where innocence is lost
And pity bleeds
I vow to raise all those who suffer from the dust
The little voice within me says I must
I have no choice!
I follow where so e'er it leads

ENSEMBLE

BABETTE.
This girl would sooner die than breathe a lie
Each word she tells
Comes from a gate of pearl
Where angels sing and saints ring bells

ARNOLD.
I think this will work
They're all confused
It's very enjoyable
I'm not often amused

JONES.
I thought he was done
But this bit of fun
Has rescued the lad
Things aren't too bad
If he had some capital –

A little capital! –
To invest in the trade
I'd make him my partner
And he would be made
PUFF, PLUNKETT, MISS CRISP, MRS GOMFIT *and* LADY
   TOODLE.
She looks so pure but Satan's lure
Is always beautiful and young
And in his gilded serpent's head
There is a golden tongue
Which with one honied kiss
Will strike you dead
TOM.
Minette!
MINETTE.
Heavens it is Tom!
TOM.
Ah such radiance!
When she is annoyed
The fire in her eyes
Sets me in flames
And my heart burns
Till I am overjoyed
Only a lover's tears could quench this fire
But it would be lit again by love's desire
MINETTE.
Ah such folly!
What drives him to this reckless deed?
He is beyond my help
I am a broken reed
That sinks to drown
Because I long
To smile at him and not to frown
Although I know that's wrong

PARSON.

In time of prayer I turn to god
I pray to him to guide me
And in my darkest hour I feel
Him standing here beside me

The sun it shines, the wind it blows
Life's spent in pain and sorrow
And what will come god only knows
To trouble us tomorrow

But if the lightning strikes you dead
My faith stays ever bright
I humbly fall upon my knees
And thank god I'm all right

The ways of man are hard to know
And god's are still more deep
But I don't worry over that
I quietly go to sleep

PUFF.

I am disturbed at the doubts cast upon my bride
Yet I hold the honour very dear
Of being president next year
And so I sacrifice myself in marriage to this cat
And call upon the prayers of every mouse and rat

ENSEMBLE

PARSON. Dearly beloved, we are gathered together here in the sight of god, and in the face of this congregation, to join together this Man and Woman in holy matrimony; which is an honourable estate, instituted by God in the time of man's innocency; signifying unto us the mystical union that is betwixt Christ and his church; which holy estate Christ adorned and beautified with his holy presence, and first miracle that he wrought, in Cana of Galilee etc etc.

ARNOLD.

Hope flies from my soul
Blood pours from my heart
Like coins from a purse
In which there's a hole
The future is dark
It could not be worse!

JONES.

He talks of pouring out his blood
He's very bold and free
With someone else's property:
His blood belongs to me

TOM.

I'd rather be bound to the stake
Than see my love bound to this sot
But we are all bound by fate
And no one can change his lot
Though she were sold as a slave
Or put on the street as a whore
Nothing I can do will change
Cruel fate's inexorable law

LOUISE.

My poor little flowers are wilted
The roses are fallen
The petals are lost
In joy we are close to sadness
In port we are tempest tossed

BABETTE.

When we were little sisters I often dreamed
That we would marry men too poor
To buy our wedding rings.
And yet in bed on our first married night
They turned into the sons of kings
Today my sister's wedding day is here

Behold the wealthy Lady Puff!
She'll eat four meals a day
(Which ought to be enough)
But she'll get little married bliss I fear

PUFF, PLUNKETT, MISS CRISP, MRS GOMFIT *and* LADY
   TOODLE.

We must breed the race
So let the marriage rites begin
God says that for this once we can do good
By giving in to sin

MINETTE.

I vow to honour and obey and trust
I say I do but mean I must
To spend my life in service to my lord
A wife who labours for her bread and board
Ring out you bells of joy!
My lover I now cast away
As all respectable young brides do
On their wedding day

The wedding rings are exchanged.

Part Two

Scene Four

Mrs Halifax's drawing-room

MINETTE *alone. She accompanies herself on a cello.*

SONG

MINETTE.
A little bird sat in a tree
Its heart was broken
The green leaves whispered
'Do not sigh: o let us sigh for you!
For we must mourn
The time is fading fast
And we must die
In that same year in which we're born'

A little bird sat in a tree
Its heart was broken
A passing cloud said
'Do not cry: o let us cry for you!
For we must turn to tears
Months grow to years
But we soon fall
And on the day we're born we die'

A knock. BABETTE *enters*

MINETTE. Babette.

They kiss.

BABETTE. I heard you were unwell. I thought perhaps your indisposition had a cause you were too shy to mention.

MINETTE. What cause Babette?

BABETTE. What does your doctor say?

MINETTE. He looks at me so strangely and shakes his head. Then he takes Puff aside and whispers to him. I ask what the doctor tells him but Puff only says: nonsense child.

BABETTE. Are you happy?

MINETTE. I have the honour to be married to the president of our society.

BABETTE. How many little Minettes will Puff be able to feed?

MINETTE. We do not discuss the farmyard here! I am a London wife. I have to discuss the German philosophers and the French encyclopaedists, follow the political situation and converse about the future of the world. I am learning the cello. I worry that I shall not be able to fulfil my wifely duties. The cello is very hard. Babette I envy your simple life at mama's side.

BABETTE. You would not envy it if you knew how poor we have become. The landlord complained and so our mistress threw us from the house. We live in a deserted hovel outside the village.

DUET

BABETTE.
The wind it blows so sharp
The rain it falls all day
The storm that blows
The rain that falls
Will wash the world away

The house is bare
We have no food

But no one shares a crust
We are alone
The world is hard as stone
And life a stony writ in dust
Yet mother rises in her bed and points above
'My child will bring us food
For she is rich in love'
MINETTE.
I live in wealth
My heart is cold
No winter storm is worse
I am both rich and poor
And young but old
And every day I curse
The gold
For which the joy of love is sold

MINETTE. Babette Lord Puff gave me this money to buy a dress to wear at our annual prayer meeting in Hyde Park. Take it. Do not thank me: what I do is wrong.

BABETTE. Goodbye poor child. Mother sends you this kiss.

BABETTE *kisses* MINETTE *and goes.*

MINETTE. I have practised till my head aches. But I dare not sleep! I dream of Tom. His dear face and his handsome bearing. It gives me such pleasure I'm sure it must be wrong.

SERENADE

TOM (*off*).
An emperor made a fair garden
Where a desolate valley had been
The flowers were rubies and diamonds
They grew on an emerald green
And in that garden he planted a tree

With leaves of tinkling jade
And I am the bird that lives in the tree
In that Eden an emperor made

Cherries of rubies! Apples of gold!
Where flowers bloom and never grow old
Where orchard boughs must not be shaken
Where the ripe peaches must not be taken
Soon I shall die in my tree of green jade
In the beautiful garden an emperor made

MINETTE. Heavens! Even when I am awake I hear his voice!
I must discuss this with Lord Puff.

A stone at the window.

MINETTE. A stone! Is the London mob again on the streets
again? How often Lord Puff is pelted as he goes on his
errands of mercy!

TOM *appears at the window, climbing onto the sill.*

MINETTE. Now I see him! It is an apparition of the London
fog. I must lie down. No no Minette, open the window. Be
brave and put it to the test! You must confront the apparition.

MINETTE *opens the window.* TOM *jumps into the room.
He wears a soldier's uniform. He is wet.*

TOM. Minette!
MINETTE. Is it really Tom?
TOM. I became a soldier to forget you. I asked to be sent to the
furthest corner of the empire. The boat slipped from the
quay. The funnel blew a long blast. Then I knew I could
not leave you! I sprang overboard. I have deserted the
queen – but I can never desert you!

MINETTE. Tom your uniform is wet. You are ruining Lord
Puff's carpet. Take it off!

TOM. Willingly. (*He starts to undress.*)

MINETTE. No no –. Better still, I think you should give
yourself up.

TOM. Never!

MINETTE. For the sake of my honour!

TOM. I don't give a damn for your honour!

MINETTE. Tom leave the room!

TOM. You are cruel!

MINETTE. You are a reckless youth!

TOM. Worse! I am an orphan!

I never kissed my mother's lips
Or laid my head upon her breast
When I was lost no father called my name
I wept – no mother came
But like a tree above a stony steep
In every wind I tremble and I weep
For as an orphan I was hurled
Into this cruel world

I was found by a missionary: a little white boy in the
African jungle.

MINETTE. Tom I love you as that missionary loved
you.

TOM. Only real love can save me! Remember the angel in my
dream!

MINETTE. Am I sent to give you the love you desire? If only
heaven would send me a sign! If only!... (*Sudden jump.*)
Ah look!

TOM. What is it?

MINETTE. My shoelace: undone! Tom that is the sign from
heaven!

TOM. Your shoelace undone?

MINETTE. Surely! A respectable woman such as I never leaves any article of her apparel undone – not even her shoelace. Tom! – heaven intends me to be your's!

TOM. O Minette promise me! I know you will keep your word.

DUET

MINETTE *and* TOM.

I promise you
When men and women love they are in paradise
What man would leave that place
What god would drive him out?
For it is paradise when lovers love
And joy is found in heaven on the ground

TOM. Minette – tonight!

MINETTE. Yes tonight! Now! Go! Suffer the just imprisonment for your desertion. Return to the world. Open a small shop. Work hard. In time you will prosper. There will be other shops. Think of it: even a small manufactory! When the years have turned us grey you will be rich enough to pay damages to Puff (by then he will be dead: the money will go to his nephew). Then I can join you with a clear heart and money in the bank.

TOM. Minette no!

> TOM *throws himself in despair at her feet. The door opens. Enter* PUFF, ARNOLD, FAWN, KEEN, PLUNKETT, MISS CRISP, MRS GOMFIT *and* LADY TOODLE.

ARNOLD. At her feet!

KEEN. Shouting her name!

MISS CRISP. In the excess of passion!

LADY TOODLE. In wet apparel!

MRS GOMFIT. With seaweed in his pocket!

PUFF. Standing on my carpet!

PLUNKETT. In a puddle!

FAWN. Disgracing his uniform!

ARNOLD. This is what she calls cello practice!

PUFF. Madam an explanation!

MINETTE. Come in dear Puff and friends. This is poor Tom. An orphan who has deserted his regiment –

ALL *except* TOM *and* MINETTE. Deserted!

MINETTE. But only for love of me, nothing more serious. We have made a pact that when you are dead dear Puff –

PUFF. Dead!

MINETTE. We all die, Puff. – then Tom will pay Arnold and set up home with me and together we will devote our evenings to the RSPR.

PUFF. I'm going to faint!

PLUNKETT. Murder her husband?

CRISP. Marry her paramour?

KEEN. Bribe her nephew-in-law to silence!

LADY TOODLE. Hide behind the respectability of the RSPR!

ARNOLD. I would like to know the full extent of the horror: how much did you mean to pay me?

MRS GOMFIT		Help!
FAWN		Police!
CRISP	*(at the window)*.	The firebrigade!
LADY TOODLE		We are hostages of a deserter!

ARNOLD *and* KEEN *seize* TOM. MRS GOMFIT *grabs his collar.* LADY TOODLE *hits him with her umbrella.*

LADY TOODLE. Scoundrel!

FAWN. Rascal!

CRISP (*to* MINETTE): Baggage!

PLUNKETT (*to* MINETTE): Jade!

PUFF. Take him back to his regiment. He must be punished.
  Minette was misled.

That pup came sniffing round her skirt
The girl is terrified and hurt
She was pursued by that young whelp
This is the time she needs my help
So my rebuke is very mild
Your sins are all forgiven child

ARNOLD (*to* PUFF): You cannot drag our name through the
  mire!

MISS CRISP. The reputation of the RSPR is at stake.

KEEN. Our enemies pounce on every scrap of scandal.

FAWN. The cause is greater than the cost.

MRS GOMFIT. Sacrifice yourself and Minette.

LADY TOODLE. Do not desert our rats.

PUFF. I have offered her forgiveness –

ARNOLD, KEEN, FAWN, PLUNKETT, MISS CRISP, MRS
  GOMFIT *and* LADY TOODLE. No never!

PUFF. – but I must give way to my friends. (*To* MINETTE:)
  Madam I divorce you!

FAWN. The police are in the street.

PLUNKETT. Take him down.

> They drag TOM out. PUFF, ARNOLD *and* MINETTE *are
> left alone.*

PUFF (*to* ARNOLD): Leave us.

ARNOLD. Not alone with this Jezebel. She twists men round
  her finger.

PUFF. Arnold I have ended in the divorce court. But there are
  rumours you will end in the court of bankruptcy.

> ARNOLD *goes.*

PUFF. A tiring day. I was looking forward to a glass of port and a quiet snooze by the fire.

MINETTE. I did not know Tom would come.

PUFF. Well well. A pity you didn't run off with him. A night out in the rain would have cured everything. You are a sensible creature. We were beginning to get comfortable and cosy. Now – they will have their divorce. A gentleman's conscience is the voice of society.

Have I done all a husband should?
Treated you with kind regard?
Paid your bills without complaint?
Loved you as I would a saint?
In health and sickness, bad and good
Been all an ideal husband should?

MINETTE. Sir I have servants and a housekeeper. You have encouraged me to learn the cello.

PUFF. Nevertheless some women would ask more.

MINETTE. Then they are selfish! If I had more I would deprive others.

PUFF. I had in mind – a certain *tendresse*.

MINETTE. You stand when I leave the room.

PUFF. Then you are satisfied?

MINETTE. I am.

PUFF. In that case ... your allowance will be more than adequate. Don't tell Arnold. Now I'll go and have my nap. You don't mind, dear, if I lock you in? There may be other deserters.

PUFF *goes. He locks the door behind him.*

MINETTE.
Strange! Tom was angry when he touched me
Yet his touch gave me such happiness
Even his shadow makes my heart leap

When he turns his dear head to look at me
I feel such joy ... and yet I am sad

SONG

Ah little bird on the tree
Tell me
Why does the bough break?
You are so light it ought to be
Easy
To take your weight

Ah little tear on that cheek
Tell me
Why do you linger there?
Because you love that face so fair?
Soon you'll
Be brushed away

Ah little wave on the sea
Say why
You toss and sigh?
The sea's too wide to care
That you're in love with it
Come to the shore
And die
And feel your pain no more

Scene Five

Divorce Court

JUDGE, COUNSEL FOR THE PROSECUTION, PUFF,
ARNOLD, MINETTE, JURY OF BIRDS. TOM *disguised as*
COUNSEL FOR THE DEFENCE.

JURY.
The geese were summoned by the fox
To be his jury
We quietly sit in his jury box
We do not ask him if the law
Defends the rich to rob the poor
That's not what he summoned us for
We do our humble duty
As citizens quack quack!

The doves were summoned by the rook
To be his jury
We swore the oath on his good book
Watch the accused and do not look
To see if the judge is the biggest crook
That's not what we were put here for
We do our humble duty
As citizens coo coo!
JUDGE.
Members of the jury!
I will impartially try this case
And show no prejudice to either side
(Although the woman's guilt could hardly be denied)
But as an English judge declare
Impartiality in the affair
It's true I share a taste in hats with one side of the case
And that we both hold bonds and stocks

In the same factories, mines and docks
And say the selfsame prayers
To ask god to protect our shares
But all the same there is no question
I favour either side in court
And I am pleased to say
An English judge cannot be bought
Or prejudiced in anyway

PROSECUTION. First witness m'lud. (ARNOLD *goes into the witness box*.) The honourable Arnold Plaice. You are the plaintiff's nephew?

ARNOLD. I am air.

PROSECUTION. Pray tell us your story.

ARNOLD. Together with other respectable members of the RSPR I found the accused convorting with a deserter from Her Majesty's army – in a posture I shudder to recall.

JUDGE. What a nice young man.

TOM. No questions m'lud.

JUDGE. I should hope not sir!

PROSECUTION. Next witness. Lord Rupert Puff CB, CMG, DL, GCMG, GCVO, ISO, KCB, KCMG and President of the RSPR.

> PUFF *goes into the witness box.*

PROSECUTION. Lord Puff before the incident in question had you any indication of the depths of your wife's depravity?

PUFF. M'lud need I answer this question?

JUDGE. Lord Puff we commend your delicacy of feeling. May I console you with the thought that whatever pain you feel will be taken into consideration when I fix the amount of damages?

PUFF. My wife once rendezvoused with a gentleman late at night on my roof-top.

JUDGE. Astonishing! It would help the court to assess the damages if we knew the full extent of your spiritual sufferings when you learned of this event.

PUFF. M'lud I hesitate again.

JUDGE. In this case silence is truly golden. (*He writes a note.*) I add a thousand pounds to the damages. You may stand down.

TOM. M'lud I have a question.

JUDGE. (*writes*). Another thousand.

TOM. Lord Puff do you come here as a husband?

PUFF. I have a marriage certificate.

TOM. It is said paper was invented by a liar. Is there a bedroom in your house?

PUFF. Several sir.

TOM. And in your bedroom is there a bed?

ARNOLD. My uncle is being harassed!

JUDGE. It is not necessary to draw the court's attention to the obvious. (*To* TOM:) I warn you sir questions come very expensive here.

TOM. And what do you do in bed?

PUFF. Sleep.

JUDGE. Well that line of questioning has come to its inevitable end.

TOM. And what else sir?

PUFF. I kneel by it to pray Almighty god to give me charity to suffer persecution with a peaceful heart.

JUDGE. What noble sentiments! (*Writes.*) A thousand pounds for mentioning god! The court will not allow this witness to be chivvied in –

TOM. M'lud –

JUDGE. (*writes*). Another thousand.

TOM. M'lud –

JUDGE (*corrects what he has written*). *Two* thousand. The court adjourns for tea.

All leave except TOM *and* MINETTE.

TOM. Minette!

MINETTE. O heavens – Tom! This is madness!

TOM. I swore to defend you to the death!

MINETTE. I thought you were in prison!

TOM. The colonel sentenced me to one hundred lashes. Puff
was his old school friend. They arranged that the last lash
would be severe enough to kill me.

MINETTE. Poor wretch!

TOM. I found out when I heard the parson laughing about it.
With your name on my lips I counted the strokes. Ninety-
six. Ninety-seven. Ninety-eight. Ninety-nine – bimbo!
The lash broke.

MINETTE. That was the hand of heaven!

TOM. They had to send to the Queen's barracks for a new
lash. (Unfortunately all our regimental lashes were too
worn out to kill a man.) The flogging was taking place in
the drawing-room of the colonel's lady. She had a migraine
and did not wish to sit in the sun. As soon as their backs
were turned I sprang through the French windows – and
here I am.

MINETTE. Where is the real barrister for the defence?

TOM. In the robing-room. I locked him in his locker.

MINETTE. There is no limit to your recklessness!

TOM. None when you are in danger!

TOM *is about to throw himself at her feet.*

MINETTE. Tom don't throw yourself at my feet! Each time
you do that my situation is made worse!

TOM.
I am the sky above your head
The earth beneath your feet
Tell me to go but I will stay!
Our lives are one – we cannot part

Unless you break your heart
In two and throw one half away

> TOM *goes to the door and listens. He returns to* MINETTE.

MINETTE. No no Tom I beg you!
TOM. Minette I must!

> TOM *throws himself at her feet. Immediately the door opens and the* JUDGE *comes in. He is followed by the* PROSECUTION, PUFF, ARNOLD *and the* JURY.

JUDGE. Madam is this how you pay your lawyer his fees?
Now I understand his heated questioning!
PROSECUTION. To think! If your lordship had not been in
such a hurry to finish the case so that you could go to the
races – all might have remained hidden!
MINETTE. Sir all is never what it seems.
JUDGE. Madam after years in court I have indeed found that
to be so. But pray do not swap potted homilies with me.
(*He makes a note.*) Two thousand.
TOM M'lud I take it the court cannot prevent me putting my
client in the witness box?
JUDGE. I find nothing in the statute books which says Jezebel
may not mount her throne – but no system of law is perfect.
(*He writes a note.*) Another thousand.

> MINETTE *goes into the witness box.*

MINETTE.
I stand before you white as driven snow
The wind may blow me whither it may go
Yet god will help a heart that's unafraid
An innocent and Christian child
Who smiles demurely and is meek and mild

TOM Madam was Lord Puff ever your husband?

MINETTE. He was most kind.

TOM. Did he – for instance – kiss you?

MINETTE. Yes sir.

TOM (*aside*): Torment! I want her to say yes and no! (*To* MINETTE:) You – gave him – satisfaction?

MINETTE. Yes sir – since it seems gentlemen take satisfaction in kissing a lady's hand.

TOM. He kissed – your mouth?

MINETTE. Yes sir at Christmas.

ARNOLD. This is crude pandering to the press!

PUFF. M'lud I have forgiven my wife. I would be grateful if this matter could be quickly ended.

ARNOLD. Madam did you allow to that deserter – (*To* TOM:) who by the way has been flogged to death: let that warn you of the power of my family – did you allow him all the privileges you allow your husband?

MINETTE. Yes.

JUDGE. Out of her mouth!

JURY. Quack quack! Coo coo!

MINETTE. More.

JUDGE *and* JURY. More!

MINETTE. He kissed my feet.

JURY. Her feet!

JUDGE. Is she mad?

TOM. M'lud the truth begins to peep out from behind the law. Far from being *paid* damages, Lord Puff should *pay* them! In church it was a marriage. By the ancient law of the bed it never was! Not once did Lord Puff do his –

The door bursts open. The DEFENCE COUNSEL *comes in. He is tied up in his gown. His wig is stuffed in his mouth.*

DEFENCE. Bla – bla – bla –

JURY. Good heavens! Quack quack! Tweet tweet!

PROSECUTION COUNSEL *releases* DEFENCE
COUNSEL.

JUDGE. Who are you?
DEFENCE. Counsel for the defence!
MINETTE (*aside*): Alas Tom is found out!
DEFENCE. I have reason to believe that man is the co-
respondent in this case!

DEFENCE COUNSEL *removes* TOM's *wig.*

ALL *except* TOM *and* MINETTE. It is he!

ENSEMBLE

JUDGE.
I'll put him in the stocks!
I'll hang him by the neck!
I'll throw him from the rocks!
I'll stretch him on the rack!
I'll burn him at the stake!
I'll drown him in the sack!
TOM. Love was my motive for this crime
A passion innocent and strong
I will not plead for clemency
And even if you pardon me
I'll do the same another time
For love can do no wrong

PUFF.
Thank god the truth is kept from sight
A secret no one will expose
I am respected at my club
Because I plucked an English rose
MINETTE.
The great love that he bears for me
Has filled him with such ecstacy
With passion wild and strong

That though he would do good to me
It drives him to do wrong.
ARNOLD.
This time the money must be mine!
But he still lives in hope
I'll spend my last few pounds to buy
A dagger and a rope
And if he wriggles out of it
I'll hang him and I'll cut his throat.
DEFENCE *and* PROSECUTION.
While I/he was getting dressed for court
This villain struck and bound me/him
He stuffed my/his wig into my/his mouth
And tied my/his gown around me/him
This makes him guilty of high treason
He should spend all his life in prison
JURY.
See in this court of English law
Truth is revealed
No crime can be concealed
Justice is blind
But sees into the secrets of the mind

JUDGE. Members of the jury I instruct you to return a verdict
   of guilty against this woman.
JURY. Guilty!
JUDGE. What a wise decision! It remains for me to fix the
   damages. (*Counts*.) dum-di-dum-di-dum-di- dum...
   One hundred and seventy-five thousand pounds.
   Court adjourned. I shall send for a military escort. (*To*
   PROSECUTION COUNSEL:) In the meantime he is in your
   custody.

   All go except TOM *and* PROSECUTION COUNSEL.

TOM. Amazing!
I prove my love is still innocent
And at that moment I lose her!

Ah woe! Ah woe! Alas!
When fate demands
What can poor creatures do
But go where it commands!

Ah woe! Ah woe! Alack!
How cruel fate has struck
When one cat is in luck
One goes into the sack

Ah woe! Ah woe! Betide!
O cruel world
In which all creatures great and small are hurled!
And tossed upon the tide
And linger for a little span
As ape or ass or man
And hurry off as quickly as they can
PROSECUTION.
I can no longer doubt!
When he was dewigged the thought stirred!
Now I am certain!

(*He goes to* TOM.)

Sir you are the long lost son of Lord Fairport.
TOM. Sir do not laugh at my misery.
PROSECUTION.
Twenty years ago the noble lord
Set sail for Biarritz in his yacht
A tempest threatened all on board
His lordship and her ladyship
Were busy saving rats

They did not think of their poor son
Until the mother cried 'What have we done?'
The nurse replied
'I left him sleeping in his cot'
Her ladyship was driven wild
Even his lordship quietly cursed his lot
He told each rat to bow its head
And from the lifeboat prow he read
The service for the dead
And then they all sang hymns to the obligato
Of a mother's tears – sforzando and staccato
And to the music of a sad chaconne
The ship turned over and was gone

On the next night a second storm hit the lifeboat and in god's wisdom all were lost.

TOM. I'm sad to hear it.

PROSECUTION. The oldest son of every Lord Fairport inherits a remarkable gift: he survives incredible dangers at the last moment. You are the Fairport son! All your history confirms it!

TOM. Why didn't my father escape?

PROSECUTION (*shrugs*). He was a second son.

TOM. What use is this to me? I have lost my treasure: Minette. I can never pay a hundred and seventy-five thousand pounds.

PROSECUTION. Sir you are the wealthiest man in England.

TOM. Ah! Go on.

PROSECUTION. But if the heir does not claim his fortune before he is twenty-one it passes to the RSPR. Sir you are twenty-one tomorrow! Which proves you are Lord Fairport!

TOM. I can pay damages and get Minette?

PROSECUTION. A drop in the ocean. (*Calls.*) M'lud!

JUDGE *comes in.*

PROSECUTION. I have found the young Lord Fairport.

JUDGE. Good heavens – so you have! I didn't recognise you in the confusion! Just like your father! We were old school friends. (*Embraces* TOM). Welcome home my lord!

TOM. I am ashamed to face my father's friend. A deserter – escaped prisoner – I shall be charged with assaulting the counsel for the defence.

JUDGE. Poo! Little matters! Chip off the old block! the scrapes your father got into! Knocking off policemen's helmets! Pushing old ladies into the Serpentine. Ha-ha-ha! Me too! Full of fun! Huh! – calls himself counsel for the defence and can't defend himself in a little fisticuffs! Wants banning from the bar! And the Lord Fairport is always colonel-in-chief of your regiment: there won't be any trouble there. As for that old maid Puff and his anarchist nephew: I shall send the papers to the director of public prosecutions. I'll have them blackballed from the club!

TRIO

TOM, JUDGE *and* PROSECUTION.
Fate's command is written in the stars and moon
He who lies in the silken cot
Has happiness and plenty for his lot
The gods of fortune do not feed
Those who only come in need
But those who bring the silver spoon

Scene Six

Mrs Halifax's drawing-room

A large sack neatly tied at the top stands upright on the floor.
BABETTE *comes in.*

BABETTE. News of my poor sister's divorce has reached
our village. I have come to comfort her and take her
home.

> MINETTE *weeps in the sack. She stays in it throughout the
> scene.*

BABETTE. Weeping but no one here!

MINETTE. Babette dearest is it you?

BABETTE. O she is in the sack! How terrible! When a cat goes
into a sack only one thing is meant!

MINETTE.
Sister I need not tell
All that has past
Its known to all the world
It made me quite unwell
The tail that was so curled
Trails on the ground
My coat has lost its sheen
My voice that used to sound
So sweet now moans
My eyes have lost their gleam

BABETTE. Sister what has happened?

MINETTE. Our mistress Mrs Halifax is too sensitive a
creature to endure the sight of my sufferings. She told the
maid to tie me in this sack and sent for the odd job man to
throw me from London bridge.

BABETTE. Quickly! We must appeal to her good nature.

MINETTE. Too late! She is too sensitive to stay in town while I am drowned. She has gone to her estate in Scotland. When she returns I will be dead.

TOM *comes in.*

TOM. Minette! Minette! I am not Tom but Lord Fairport! We are rich! I shall pay Puff damages and have the pleasure of damaging him again on the nose!

BABETTE. Lower your voice sir.

TOM. What is the matter?

MINETTE. Alas!

TOM. O god – in the sack!

BABETTE. Mrs Halifax has spoken.

MINETTE. It is fate.

TOM. O horror! I shall throw myself into the river with you!

MINETTE. I cannot be the innocent cause of your destruction! Live and be happy!

TOM. Command me to live – but happiness you cannot command!

MINETTE. In time the wound will heal.

BABETTE (*weeps*). How noble! The loss to the world!

MINETTE. Is my sister crying?

TOM. She is.

MINETTE. Then comfort her.

TRIO

TOM.
Babette all hearts are moved
By the vision of you crying
You sob so prettily
On learning that your sister's dying

(*Aside:*).
How like Minette she is!
Even simpler – more gentle – pretty!
What is this chaos in my heart?
A joy that fights with pity
I think I am in love with her
But I must hold her to make sure

> *He holds* BABETTE.

O little sister do not cry
You will feel better by and by
The pearls upon your little face
Are jewels of the feline race
BABETTE.
His touch is gentle soft and kind
The pain is rushing from my mind
A secret bliss begins! It stirs!
I wish that he were mine not her's
TOM.
What strange ideas are in my head?
With two desires I am torn
The moment one old love is dead
A greater sweeter love is born
MINETTE.
O what do I hear?
TOM.
Minette I cannot lie to you
If you could live I'd die for you
But since your death has been decreed
You can't give what all young men need
Your sister's precious in my sight
I hope you'll say that it's all right?
Minette believe me it is true
I love her since she's so like you

MINETTE.
In life we have one aim to seek
Forgive and turn the other cheek
Place on her cheek that kiss divine
That once you longed to place on mine
If I can join you two today
My life has not been thrown away
TOM *and* BABETTE.
How noble!
MINETTE.
With this good deed I quit this place
A voice in heaven calls
'Arise o sacrifice of love!'
A hand unties my sack
And through the little patch of blue above
I fly
On earth a cat
But now a spotless dove!

DUET

TOM *and* BABETTE.
I promise you!
And with this kiss I vow
That I will always love you as I love you now!

Love stays the planets on their course
And over tides holds sway
And in its plan
It keeps a little place for man

BABETTE. Today mother loses a daughter but gains a son!
TOM. And riches! And grandchildren! Minette we shall name our firstborn after you.

MINETTE. It might be a boy.

TOM. Nevertheless! – it shall be called Minette. All our children will be honoured with the name of their aunt.

BABETTE. We promise you!

MINETTE *and* BABETTE (*they kiss through the sack*). O sister!

TOM. Minette let me throw myself at your feet in a last farewell!

MINETTE. O no Tom please don't!

> TOM *throws himself at* MINETTE's *feet. The door opens. Enter* ARNOLD, PUFF, KEEN, FAWN, PLUNKETT, MISS CRISP, MRS GOMFIT *and* LADY TOODLE.

ARNOLD. See! Even when the wretched woman is in the sack he paws her!

No one is safe
He'll take all we've got
Lock stock and barrel
He'll take the lot

PUFF. Lord Fairport retarded congratulations on your rescue as an infant. The great wealth you inherit was clearly intended for our friends the rats. Then why has god tempted you in this way? So that you may win greater merit by renouncing your fortune. As president of the RSPR I have come to accept your gift.

ALL *except* MINETTE, BABETTE *and* TOM.

No man can take his money to the grave
Death is mightier than greed
But he lies richly in the dust who gave
All he was worth
To those in need
While he still walked on earth

TOM.

No sir I will not part with my wealth

I have been poor and rich
Lost and found
In love and out of love
And in love again
Now I have this to say

While rats depend on cats
There is no hope for rats
Only when rat helps rat
Will rats be free
Till then cats feed on rats
And call it charity

TOM *and* BABETTE. Minette farewell!

TOM *and* BABETTE *go.*

ARNOLD. He's an impostor!

PUFF. He's rich enough to prove he isn't ten times over!

KEEN. Something must be done!

FAWN. Don't let him get away with it!

CRISP. Robber!

MRS GOMFIT. Thief!

PLUNKETT. A sorry day!

LADY TOODLE. I shall have hysterics! My money! My money! My money!

LOUISE (*holds out a collecting box*).
Out from its hole a little mouse
Crept into this cruel –

PLUNKETT (*clips Louise round the ear*). Shut up!

MISS CRISP. Not now for god's sake!

FAWN. Send her back to the sewer!

KEEN. You'll get bitten my girl!

LADY TOODLE. My money! My money!

PUFF. I am tired and I was looking forward to a quiet evening in my slippers. I suppose the president must take the lead.

Lord Fairport has gone to his lawyers to make his will.
That must be stopped.

ALL *except* MINETTE.

In doing right we are allowed
To do a little wrong
How else can goodness triumph
Where the wicked are so strong?

All go except for MINETTE. *She is alone in the sack.*

MINETTE. Alone? Then I wait quietly for the odd job man.

I sink into the water
The sackcloth wound about me
I sink still deeper in the dark
Strange creatures swim around me!

I part from life without regret – adieu!
I have hurt none and I have helped a few
When I lie on the bottom of the sea
Those few will sometimes think of me

Down slowly down
How gracefully I turn
Round slowly round
One final dance
To rest upon the bottom of the deep
And with a little bow
I fall asleep

Scene Seven

The Temple – Lawyer's Chambers

PROSECUTION COUNSEL *and* TOM.

PROSECUTION. My lord I have made your will. Your fortune passes to Miss Babette on your demise.

TOM (*quietly reflective*). What a strange life I have led

Man makes his world and makes himself
In time all shall free
The fight is hard yet this shall be
As rocks are turned to sand along the shore
By the unceasing hammer of the sea

The stars and planets turn in iron laws
And nothing changes in a million years
The harmony or discord of the spheres
But man is not the creature of this plan
The fate of man is man.
PROSECUTION (*calls*): Lucian.

> LUCIAN *enters.*

PROSECUTION. Lucian is my clerk. He will witness your signature. Sign my lord.

> TOM *stoops over the table to sign the will.* LUCIAN *stabs him in the back.*

TOM. O.

> TOM *falls to* LUCIAN's *feet. The door slowly opens. Enter* PUFF, ARNOLD, KEEN, FAWN, PLUNKETT, MISS CRISP, MRS GOMFIT *and* LADY TOODLE.

PUFF. Dear me. I see Lord Fairport has committed suicide.

ARNOLD. In grief at losing Minette.

LUCIAN. Tried to swallow poison. I struggled with him. He fell on the office paper-knife. As you see, he is beyond saving. Excuse me.

He wipes blood from his hands on the will. Then tears it up.

PROSECUTION. As the noble lord dies intestate the money passes to the RSPR. But the legal expenses will be considerable.

PUFF. We shall be happy to pay since we can now afford to. At last I can go to bed.

PROSECUTION *and* LUCIAN.
In cases of this sort we charge enormous fees
We never listen to our clients' pleas
We suck their blood and when their veins run dry
We do not listen to their groans
We suck the marrow from their bones

ALL.
The truth shall triumph upon earth
God casts the evil into flames
And pays the dead in gold
According to their worth

We help the hungry rats
Teach them to respect the cats
We cast one drop of rain
And a few seeds
Upon the desert of their needs
And by such deeds
We hope to save the world again

BABETTE *runs in. As she sings the others, except* TOM, *leave.*

BABETTE. Ah Tom is it true?
  The news will kill mother
  She has gained and lost a son in one day

LAMENT

Our happiness was too great for the world
The jealous winds have blown his life over the ocean
The flowers have stolen his breath
The nightingale has stolen his voice
The honeysuckle has stolen his arms
The sea has drunk his tears and become a love potion
The envious ground takes his body and becomes immortal
The earth takes his life and overcomes death.

    BABETTE *goes*. MINETTE's *ghost appears*. TOM *reaches towards it.*

DUET

TOM.
Ah Minette at last we meet in death
MINETTE.
Ah that is often said
But here we are too old
TOM.
Your hand is cold
MINETTE.
The warmth is fading from your lips
TOM.
My sighs will give you breath
MINETTE.
No more than cold winds on the shore
TOM.
My kiss will raise you from the dead

MINETTE.
That too is often said
TOM.
But I would die for you
MINETTE.
Poor Tom can die no more
TOM.
Will we never love again?
MINETTE.
You leave love in the world of pain
TOM.
Love lives forever
MINETTE.
No never
TOM.
I will follow where you go
MINETTE.
And now we part
TOM.
My heart says no
MINETTE.
Yet it is so

    MINETTE *goes as* TOM *dies.* LOUISE *comes on.*

LOUISE. All gone! O Tom – they have killed him! And he was the best of them! I see they cannot be trusted! One day when they are hungry they will eat me.

    She opens her collecting box and steals the money.

With this I can return to my old life! I have lived with cats and studied their ways! Now I shall have a chance to survive.

    She puts a coin in TOM's *pocket.*

A coin. Perhaps even now Tom may need it.

SONG

I have become a mouse again
I'll steal the milk and rob the grain
My teeth are sharp and I can bite
I'll give the ladies such a fright
They'll stand upon their chairs and yell
I'll be a little fiend from hell
      Screech! Screech!

RESTORATION

The music

Given here are the melodies composed by Nick Bicât for the play. Full orchestration can be obtained from Nigel Brittain, London Management & Representation Ltd, 235 Regent Street, London W1.

ROSES (BOB)

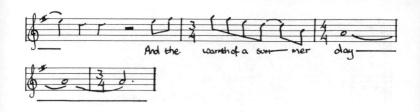

And the warmth of a summer day

SONG OF LEARNING (FRANK)

1. For fif-ty thous-and years I ⌠ lived in a shack I
⌡ hammered and toiled
⌊ followed the plough The

learned a shack is not a place to live in _____ For
All I made was ta-ken a-way _____ from my hands
food I ate was left by the beasts _____ of the field

fif-ty thou-sand years I ⌠ built mansions for men of wealth
⌡ ran fac-tries for men of wealth
⌊ dug gar-dens for men of wealth

That's how I learned to ⌠ build a man-sion for my-self
⌡ run a fac-try for my-self
⌊ dig a gar-den for my-self

3. For 4. For

fif-ty thou-sand years | waited at ta — ble——
                       | fought in their wars ——

learned to cook and how to un — bot-tle the wine   For
died so of-ten | learned—— how to sur-vive   For

fif-ty thou-sand years | watched rich men tuck in like swine
                       | fought battles to save their wealth

From now on the grub is gon-na be all—— mine ——
that's how I learned to loathe the en — e — my my——self——

5. } For fif-ty thou-sand years | printed their books
6. } | gave them my life   But in

learned to read by look-ing ov-er their shoul-der   For
all that time they ne-ver learned how to live ——   For

fif-ty thou-sand years I built   li-braries for men of   wealth ——
was go-verned by men of   wealth ——

That's how I learned to write the books I need my-self ——
Now I have learned to make the laws up for my-self ——

I have known pain and bowed be-fore bea-uty shared in joy and died ——
—— in du-ty Fif-ty thou-sand years I lived well——

I learned how to blow up your   hell.

DREAM (ROSE)

At night I pass though the land un-seen Though you lie a-wake
To coda

My smile is as sharp— as the blade in my hand—

But when the fire is spent the ground is not scorched the trees are not

charred The land— is fresh in the mor— ning dew—

The ca-ttle went though the flames yet are— not dead—

On-ly the white—man's bones are black ly-ing by his burned out.

banks Now cat-tle graze by the ri-ver banks-

Men and wo-men work— in— the fields —

All they grow they own To be shared by young and old

In the eve-ning they rest And the song of free-dom is sung

I am

CODA

The ven-om does not kill the snake.

THE WOOD SONG (MOTHER)

The wood-en cra-dle— the wood-en spoon the wood-en ta-ble— The wood-en
bed— The wood-en house the wood-en beam The wood-en pul-pit the wood-en
bench The wood-en ham-mer the wood-en stair The wood-en gal-ows the wood-en
box The iron chain the brass lock The hu-man toil— the earthly span—
These are the lot of eve-ry man— The winds that drive the storms that blast for
eve-ry man the die is cast All you— who would re-sist your fate strike

8va keyboard plays solo from
8va until faded.

SONG OF THE CALF (BOB)

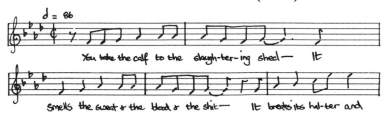

You take the calf to the slaugh-ter-ing shed— It
smells the sweat & the blood & the shit— It breaks its hal-ter and

but-cher a — gain   6. For thogh it will run and
bell-ow and rear — The calf will be tied to the slaughter house door The
but-cher will cut its throat with his knife It will sink to its knees and
lose   its life   7. The morning's o — — ver —
the work is done   You eat and drink
and have your fun   The but-cher is —
sharp-en-ing his knife to — day   Do you know, do you
care,   who will get a — way?

A MAN GROANS (ROSE AND MOTHER)

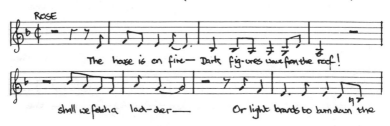

ROSE

The house is on fire — Dark fig-ures wave from the roof!
shall we fetch a lad-der — Or light brands to burn down the

THE GENTLEMAN (BOB AND ROSE)

who would raise their voice when soft words will do— my friend?

why use a knife— when a smile makes— cuts that

bleed?— When you have the mind—— why——

both—er to chop off the head? When white hands will—

—— do the work why make your hands— feel——

SONG OF TALKING (FRANK AND BOB)

♩ = 92 FRANK + BOB (unison)

1. My mate was a hard case Worked be-side him on the bench for

years Hard-ly said a word Talk-ing isn't ea-sy When the ma—

—chines run One day he dropped a coin He un-screwed the safe-ty

rail to get it back The press ham-mer struck his head I

nursed him on the con-crete floor He looked up at the roof and

said   The green hills by the sea Where the light shines Through tall dark

pines ——————   A min-ute lat-er he was

dead   2. Did-n't speak ev-en on the street   Once I

saw him shop-ping with his wife   He on-ly nod-ded   He was de-cent to

me   But I'd heard ru-mours   He'd done time in

cho-key   And his fist   could   hit you like a steel-capped boot

Then he un-screwed the safe-ty rail   I nursed him on the con-crete

floor   He looked up at the roof and said   The green hills by the

sea   in the dark grove I first made love ——————

A min-ute lat-er he was   dead

3. You did-n't pick a row with him   Once I bumped him on the park-ing

lot   No real da-mage   He stared thru' the wind-screen Then drove off

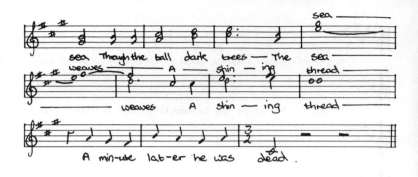

sea Though the tall dark trees — The sea
weaves — A — shin — ing thread
—— weaves A shin — ing thread —
A min-ute lat-er he was dead.

LEGEND OF GOOD FORTUNE (MOTHER)

Men lived in peace and plen-ty When the world was as young as the

day But a god came down from heav—en And

took the good things a —way He put them all in a

bas-ket And slow-ly climbed up to his cave He

put the bas-ket un-der his head and slept like a wea-ry

slave There— passed on earth ten

a-ges of war Men groaned and lived as the dead when this

SONG OF THE CONJOUROR (ROSE AND BOB)

white They screamed as they watched him strug-gle and-

— thrash With horror they saw him sink-ing

down And stood on the bank to watch him drown.

TREE OF LIBERTY (ROSE AND FRANK)

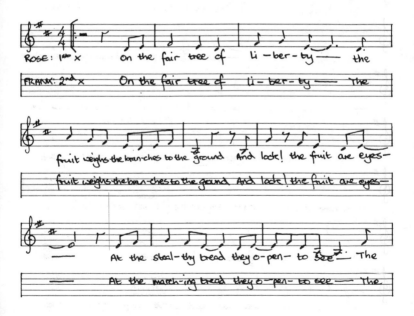

ROSE: 1ʳᵈ x   On the fair tree of li-ber-ty —— the

FRANK: 2ⁿᵈ x   On the fair tree of li-ber-ty —— The

fruit weighs the bran-ches to the ground And look! the fruit are eyes—

fruit weighs the bran-ches to the ground And look! the fruit are eyes—

—— At the steal-thy bread they o-pen-to see—. The

—— At the march-ing bread they o-pen-to see —— The

strike   like thun—der bolts   The rest are re-freshed in its cool

—   green— shade

FRANK + ROSE   And

so the fair tree grows—   As tall as the pine and as strong

—   as the oak—   Wreathed with the wild rose— & the hang-ing vine

—   As our fore-fa-thers spoke and so the fair tree grows—

—   As   tall   as the pine and as strong—

—   as the oak—   Wreathed with the wild rose r the hang-ing vine

—   As our fore-fa-thers spoke.

SUDDENLY (BOB)

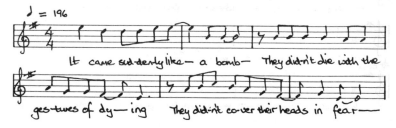

♩ = 196

It came sud-den-ly like— a bomb—   They did-n't die with the

ges-tures of dy—ing   They did-n't co-ver their heads in fear—

THE DRUM SONG (BOB)

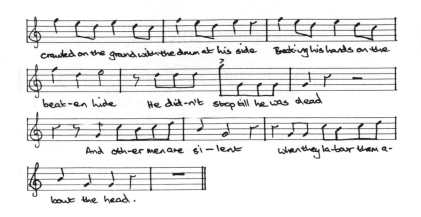

crawled on the ground with the drum at his side   Beating his hands on the

beat-en hide   He did-n't stop till he was dead

And oth-er men are si — lent   when they la-bour them a-

bout the head.

MAN IS WHAT HE KNOWS (ROSE)

Does the judge say I send your arms to pri-son to-day But your

feet are free— To walk a-way? Does the boss buy the a-pple

core from the mar-ket stall and   leave the skin ?   He

buys it all— Do the troops shoot to kill your sto-mach but not your head? They

shoot to kill— You drop down dead Once   sa-tan roamed the earth

— to find — souls that he could buy — Nashe comes to steel

— your mind He doesn't wait till you die — The
hous-es burn on the edge of town It's on-ly the dawn we can tell
— when it rea-ches your house you will fight like the
men locked in their cell — Man is what he
knows or doesn't know — Some men reap
on-ly death and sow fam-ine where-e-ver they march But
they do not own the earth — Soon-er be-lieve I could strike
— it a blow with my fist And
miss Geese fly — o-ver the moon + ne-ver
know — that for a mo — ment They fill the world with beau-ty —
Flakes fall — in the snow Not know-ing where they fall But
each flake falls to the world be-low — And in the

morn-ing is part of the beau—ti-ful rai—ment of snow The wind ca-nnot tell where it may blow But Men may know who they are and wither they go—

Details of some other books published by Methuen on the modern theatre are given on the following pages.

If you would like to receive, free of charge, regular information about new plays and theatre books from Eyre Methuen, please send your name and address to:

The Marketing Department (Drama)
Methuen London Ltd
North Way
Andover
Hampshire SP10 5BE

Methuen's Modern Plays

Jean Anouilh	*Antigone*
	Becket
	The Lark
John Arden	*Serjeant Musgrave's Dance*
	The Workhouse Donkey
	Armstrong's Last Goodnight
John Arden and	*The Business of Good Govecnment*
Margaretta D'Arcy	*The Royal Pardon*
	The Hero Rises Up
	The Island of the Mighty
	Vandaleur's Folly
Wolfgang Bauer,	*Shakespeare the Sadist,*
Rainer Werner	
Fassbinder,	*Bremen Coffee,*
Peter Handke,	*My Foot My Tutor,*
Franz Xaver Kroetz	*Stallerhof*
Brendan Behan	*The Quare Fellow*
	The Hostage
	Richard's Cork Leg
Edward Bond	*A-A-America !* and *Stone*
	Saved
	Narrow Road to the Deep North
	The Pope's Wedding
	Lear
	The Sea
	Bingo
	The Fool and *We Come to the River*
	Theatre Poems and Songs
	The Bundle
	The Woman
	The Worlds with *The Activists Papers*
	Restoration and *The Cat*
	Summer
Bertolt Brecht	*Mother Courage and Her Children*
	The Caucasian Chalk Circle
	The Good Person of Szechwan
	The Life of Galileo
	The Threepenny Opera
	Saint Joan of the Stockyards
	The Resistible Rise of Arturo Ui
	The Mother
	Mr Puntila and His Man Matti
	The Measures Taken and other Lehrstücke
	The Days of the Commune
	The Messingkauf Dialogues
	Man Equals Man and *The Elephant Calf*
	The Rise and Fall of the City of Mahagonny and *The Seven Deadly Sins*
	Baal
	A Respectable Wedding and other one-act plays
	Drums in the Night
	In the Jungle of Cities

	The Homecoming
	Tea Party and other plays
	Landscape and *Silence*
	Old Times
	No Man's Land
	Betrayal
	The Hothouse
Luigi Pirandello	*Henry IV*
	Six Characters in Search of an Author
Stephen Poliakoff	*Hitting Town* and *City Sugar*
David Rudkin	*The Sons of Light*
	The Triumph of Death
Jean-Paul Sartre	*Crime Passionnel*
Wole Soyinka	*Madmen and Specialists*
	The Jero Plays
	Death and the King's Horseman
C P Taylor	*And a Nightingale Sang . . .*
	Good
Nigel Williams	*Line 'Em*
	Class Enemy
Charles Wood	*Veterans*
Theatre Workshop	*On What a Lovely War*
Various authors	*Best Radio Plays of 1978* (Don Haworth: *Episode on a Thursday Evening*; Tom Mallin: *Halt! Who Goes There?*; Jennifer Phillips: *Daughters of Men*; Fay Weldon: *Polaris*; Jill Hyem: *Remember Me*; Richard Harris: *Is it Something I Said?*)
	Best Radio Plays of 1979 (Shirley Gee: *Typhoid Mary*; Carey Harrison: *I Never Killed My German*; Barrie Keeffe: *Heaven Scent*; John Kirkmorris: *Coxcomb*; John Peacock: *Attard in Retirement*; Olwen Wymark: *The Child*)
	Best Radio Plays of 1980 (Stewart Parker: *The Kamkaze Ground Staff Reunion Dinner*; Martyn Read: *Waving to a Train*; Peter Redgrave: *Martyr of the Hives*; William Trevor: *Beyond the Pale*)

Methuen's New Theatrescripts

This series aims to close the gap between the appearance of new plays in the theatre and their publication in script form, and to make available new and unconventional work which might otherwise not appear in print

MICHAEL ABBENSETTS
Samba

ANDREY AMALRIK
East-West & Is Uncle Jack a Conformist?

HOWARD BRENTON
Sore Throats & Sonnets of Love and Opposition
Thirteenth Night & A Short Sharp Shock!

ANTON CHEKHOV
The Seagull (*A new version by Thomas Kilroy*)
DAVID CREGAN
Poor Tom & Tina
DAVID EDGAR
Teendreams
Wreckers
DAVID HALLIWELL
The House
BARRIE KEEFFE
Frozen Assets
Sus
Bastard Angel
HANIF KUREISHI
Borderline
DAVID LAN
Sergeant Ola and his Followers
STEPHEN LOWE
Touched
Tibetan Inroads
JOHN MACKENDRICK
Lavender Blue & Noli Me Tangere
DAVID MAMET
American Buffalo & Sexual Perversity in Chicago
& Duck Variations
MUSTAPHA MATURA
Nice, Rum An' Coca Cola & Welcome Home Jacko
MICHAEL MEYER
Lunatic and Lover
STEPHEN POLIAKOFF
Shout Across the River
Strawberry Fields
American Days
The Summer Party
DENNIS POTTER
Brimstone and Treacle
PETER WHELAN
The Accrington Pals
NIGEL WILLIAMS
Sugar and Spice & Trial Run
CHARLES WOOD
Has 'Washington' Legs & Dingo

The Master Playwrights

Collections of plays by the best-known modern playwrights in value-for-money paperbacks
John Arden
PLAYS: ONE
Serjeant Musgrave's Dance, The Workhouse Donkey, Armstrong's Last Goodnight

Brendan Behan
THE COMPLETE PLAYS
The Hostage, The Quare Fellow, Richard's Cork Leg, Moving Out,
A Garden Party, The Big House

Edward Bond
PLAYS: ONE
Saved, Early Morning, The Pope's Wedding
PLAYS: TWO
Lear, The Sea, Narrow Road to the Deep North, Black Mass, Passion

Noel Coward
PLAYS: ONE
Hay Fever, The Vortex, Fallen Angels, Easy Virtue
PLAYS: TWO
Private Lives, Bitter Sweet, The Marquise, Post-Mortem
PLAYS: THREE
Design for Living, Cavalcade, Conversation Piece, and Hands Across
the Sea, Still Life and Fumed Oak from Tonight at 8.30
PLAYS: FOUR
Blithe Spirit, This Happy Breed, Present Laughter, and Ways and
Means, The Astonished Heart and 'Red Peppers' from Tonight at
8.30

Henrik Ibsen
Translated and introduced by Michael Meyer
PLAYS: ONE
Ghosts, The Wild Duck, The Master Builder
PLAYS: TWO
A Doll's House, An Enemy of the People, Hedda Gabler
PLAYS: THREE
Rosmersholm, Little Eyolf, The Lady from the Sea
PLAYS: FOUR
John Gabriel Borkman, The Pillars of Society, When We Dead
Awaken

Joe Orton
THE COMPLETE PLAYS
Entertaining Mr Sloane, Loot, What the Butler Saw, The Ruffian on
the Stair, The Erpingham Camp, Funeral Games, The Good and
Faithful Servant

Harold Pinter
PLAYS: ONE
The Birthday Party, The Room, The Dumb Waiter, A Slight Ache,
A Night Out
PLAYS: TWO
The Caretaker, Night School, The Dwarfs, The Collection, The
Lover, five revue sketches
PLAYS: THREE
The Homecoming, Tea Party, The Basement, Landscape, Silence, six
revue sketches
PLAYS: FOUR
Old Times, No Man's Land, Betrayal, Monologue, Family Voices

Terence Rattigan
PLAYS: ONE
French Without Tears, The Winslow Boy, The Browning Version, Harlequinade

Strindberg
THE FATHER, MISS JULIE, THE GHOST SONATA
PLAYS: TWO
The Dance of Death, A Dream Play, The Stronger
Introduced and translated by Michael Meyer

J. M. Synge
THE COMPLETE PLAYS
In the Shadow of the Glen, Riders to the Sea, The Tinker's Wedding, The Well of the Saints, The Playboy of the Western World, Deirdre of the Sorrows

Oscar Wilde
THREE PLAYS
Lady Windermere's Fan, An Ideal Husband, The Importance of Being Earnest